Martin Boot

T0270231

111 Places for Kids in Bristol That You Shouldn't Miss

Photographs by Barbara Evripidou

emons:

For Lois and Mersina,
my proud little Bristolians
Martin Booth

For Theo and Anna
Barbara Evripidou

© Emons Verlag GmbH
© Photographs: © Barbara Evripidou, except:
Planet Ice (ch. 76): photo by Martin Booth
Wildflower Meadow (ch. 105): photo by Simon Hill
© Cover motif: Mauritius shutterstock.com/Sion Hannuna; Edinburghcitymom;
Evgeny Atamanenko; Nataliia Pyzhova; Lithiumphoto
Layout: Editorial Design & Artdirection, Conny Laue,
based on a design by Lübbeke | Naumann | Thoben and Nina Schäfer
Maps: velovia, www.velovia.bike
Frank Ullrich & Kristof Halasz
© OpenStreetMap contributors
Edited by Ros Horton
Printing and binding: Grafisches Centrum Cuno, Calbe
Printed in Germany 2023
ISBN 978-3-7408-1665-0
First edition

Guidebooks for Locals & Experienced Travellers
Join us in uncovering new places around the world at
www.111places.com

FOREWORD

On an autumnal Sunday afternoon, my seven-year-old daughter Lois and I decided to go for an explore. We usually spend most of our time on bicycles, but this afternoon we were on foot, making our way up Brandon Hill to climb the narrow spiral staircase of the Cabot Tower. From the top, there is one of the best views of the city that we call home, having both been born in the same hospital 33 years apart.

Peering out from this unrivalled vantage point, Lois spotted not just our flat but also the SS *Great Britain*, We The Curious planetarium and Underfall Yard, just three places where we have spent many happy hours with Lois' older sister Mersina; and where I hope that you will too after reading about these family friendly treasures here in this book, whether you also call Bristol home or are visiting for the first time.

If you can't hitch a ride in one of the hot air balloons that are a regular sight in the summer, I highly recommend either climbing to the top of the Cabot Tower or the Wills Memorial Building, both offering you phenomenal panoramas of Bristol stretching out like an intricate jigsaw below. Look beyond the city boundaries and you'll see that it swiftly becomes the countryside at its outer edges. But the natural world permeates into the urban landscape, with we Bristolians sharing our neighbourhoods with badgers, foxes and even a few birds of prey.

In the course of writing this book, I have had the privilege of seeing Bristol once again through child's eyes. And what a place to be a child Bristol is! What a place to explore. From gymnastics in Hartcliffe to street art in Bedminster, circus in St Paul's to secret vaults in Clifton, skating in an old swimming pool in Bishopsworth to eating pakoras in Easton, these chapters will take you on new adventures across a wonderful city. The story of Bristol will become your story as you make memories to last a lifetime.

Martin Booth

111 PLACES

1_ AHH TOOTS

Where cakes look almost too good to eat

Is it possible to walk by Ahh Toots without being lured in by their window display? It's always fit to bursting with baked delights that some people say look too good to be eaten. But don't be silly! You would be missing out on some of the finest and most delicious delicacies in town that are all made here in this 'cakery and biscuitier' where laptops are banned and decadence is encouraged.

A typical window display might include the likes of a ginger and miso caramel cake, treacle tart, chocolate stacked cookies, carrot and courgette cake, salted caramel brownies, Lotus blondies, rocky roads, flapjacks, croissant cake, friands, Oreo mint brownies and rhubarb frangipanis. Think you've made your mind up? That babka on the counter looks tempting too.

If We The Curious (see ch. 37) is at the intersection between art and science, Ahh Toots is at the intersection between art and cake. Each creation made by Tam Galliford, Amy Symonds and their small team is an individual work of art.

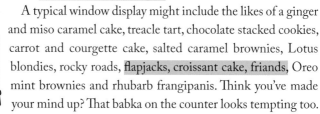

> **TIP:** A metal firemark on the front of Ahh Toots is a reminder of when insurance companies' fire brigades only put out the fires of businesses insured with them.

Within a Tudor-fronted building on one of Bristol's oldest streets, Ahh Toots feels as if it has been here for ever. But, in fact, it only opened in 2020 in what was previously Bristol's oldest fish and chip shop. Before that they were based at St Nick's Market for six years. Look for an engraving of their original stall on one of the bookshelves in the cosy seating area at the back of the café as you enjoy a cake and contemplate whether you should have one more slice. Of course you should.

Address 17 Christmas Street, BS1 5BT, + 44 (0)117 9277099, www.ahhtoots.com // Getting there 5-minute walk from fountains // Hours Wed – Fri 8am – 5pm, Sat 10am – 5pm // Ages 4+

2_ AIRHOP

Let off steam on trampolines

Get ready: you're standing on a small platform in the Wipeout Zone, about to begin. You're imagining jumping over the lower spinning arm and ducking underneath the higher arm as they head towards you one after the other in an unknown direction. Will you get wiped out? Probably. But that's half the fun! Compete against friends and family to see who can remain standing for the longest, and try not to laugh too much when your little sister goes flying into the air, or is somehow carried on the arm to the neighbouring platform.

Almost 150 interconnecting trampolines take up most of the space on the floor, and even up some of the walls here, but, like the Wipeout Zone, there are plenty of other activities to get stuck into. Race through the obstacle course, play dodgeball, whack your opponent with a pugil stick on the battle beams, or use a trampoline to do a leaping slam-dunk.

As you might expect, safety is of paramount importance, with jumping areas within the park supervised at all times by AirHop staff who are quick to make sure that the strict safety rules are adhered to while, of course, allowing those taking part to have loads of fun.

Birthday parties are popular here, with party-goers getting their own rooms for the all-important pizza, slushies, cake and even unlimited squash if you're lucky. For the littlest bouncers, AirHop's regular 'Mini Hoppers' sessions for children aged six months to six years give them free rein around most of the space, with the two hours ending with bubbles!

Address Unit 5, Britannia Road, Patchway, BS34 5TA, +44 (0)808 5038996, www.airhop-bristol.com // Getting there 10-minute walk from Mall at Cribbs Causeway // Hours Mon & Fri 10am–7pm, Tue, Wed & Thu 3–7pm, Sat, school and Bank Holidays 9am–7pm, Sun 9am–6pm // Ages 6 months+

TIP: Watch a movie at Vue and bowl at Hollywood Bowl in Cribbs Causeway.

3_ ALL-ABOARD WATERSPORTS

Learn the ropes

One of the classic picture-postcard views of Bristol is from close to the Cottage Inn looking across the Floating Harbour to the Balamory-style houses on the hill in Cliftonwood. The view will be made even better with the addition of multicoloured sails from a variety of boats – most likely from All-Aboard Watersports, a charity that has been operating in the docks for almost 50 years.

It's not just sailing either, with kayaking, rowing, canoeing and stand-up paddleboarding also available. You might not know your port from your poop deck or your starboard from your stern, but you'll soon be mastering the basics of sailing; following in the footsteps of merchants and even pirates in days gone by who left these very docks for nautical adventures across the globe. Just be prepared to get wet!

Have you heard of a KataKanu? All-Aboard Watersports has a fleet of these vessels: brilliantly innovative and versatile craft created by joining two kayaks in a catamaran formation, which can seat up to six paddlers at the same time. Total beginners can also take to the water in Hansa sailing boats that can accommodate either one or two people, as well as the more familiar kayaks or paddleboards, a particularly leisurely way to navigate the harbour.

Courses for children run by All-Aboard Watersports include after-school and holiday sailing clubs. Perhaps you will first take to the water in a dinghy or single- or double-hander in Bristol, and in a few years' time be representing Team GB at the Olympic Games.

Address Baltic Wharf, Cumberland Road, Spike Island, BS1 6XG, +44 (0)117 9290801, www.allaboardwatersports.co.uk // Getting there Short walk from Underfall Yard; bus M2 to Spike Island // Hours Mon–Fri 9am–3pm // Ages 8+

TIP: Grab a bite to eat on the top deck of the Grain Barge.

4_ASHTON COURT MINIATURE RAILWAY

Toot–toot!

Whether it's a high-speed GWR intercity or a steam-powered locomotive, there is always a wide choice of trains on which to ride at the Ashton Court Miniature Railway. Most trains are powered by steam, and most of the volunteers driving them are powered by copious amounts of tea and coffee. Despite being scaled-down versions of the real thing, the trains here – be they steam, electric or diesel models – are beautifully authentic, if you find beauty in, for example, the London & North Eastern Railway Thompson Class B1.

Each train runs around two different tracks – one at ground level and one slightly raised, but both around a third of a mile long taking passengers through woodland and into a tunnel. Your driver will most likely be the person who has built the train you are travelling on, and will be happy to answer any questions. Tickets are not expensive, giving you plenty of opportunities to ride on as many different locomotives as possible.

In 2019, there was uproar as Bristol City Council threatened to withdraw the lease of the four-acre site that the railway is on from the Bristol Society of Model & Experimental Engineers, who have been here since 1972, but according to the council do not make them enough money. Thankfully, good sense prevailed, and you will continue to get the most reliable, most punctual and the friendliest train service in the city here at Ashton Court.

TIP: Bring a picnic to enjoy on the grass at Ashton Court.

Address Ashton Court, BS8 3PX, +44 (0)117 9467110, www.bristolmodelengineers.co.uk/public-running-days // Getting there Plenty of cycle racks next to the Golf Café; bus X3 or X4 // Hours Regular weekends from Mar–Dec (check website for details) // Ages 2+

5_AVON VALLEY RAILWAY

Step back in time with the sound of steam

Is that sound you hear the excited scream of a train-mad toddler or a steam engine in full throttle? It's sometimes hard to know, with so much happening at Bitton railway station! The Midland Railway could have been lost for ever when it was closed in the 1960s, but thanks to a group of enthusiastic volunteers, three miles of track has been relaid, locomotives and carriages restored, and the sounds of steam (and toddlers) have returned.

In the heatwaves of 2022, diesel services replaced the restored steam locomotives some days due to fears of fires beside the line. But for enthusiasts, these diesel services can be just as exciting as steam – and they pull the same heritage carriages anyway on services to Oldland Common or Avon Riverside. If you want to ride in even more style, you can upgrade to first class.

Throughout the year, there are also plenty of special events. A restored locomotive from the Fry's chocolate factory in nearby Keynsham runs at Easter, teddy bears' picnic weekends see free travel for children who bring their teddy bear, and there are special visits from Father Christmas during November and December.

Even if there are no trains running along the line when you visit, you can still take a look around the beautifully restored Victorian station and goods yard, go for a walk or cycle alongside the track, get a souvenir from the gift shop, and have a bite to eat from the buffet where you can sit and enjoy your chicken nuggets and chips in a converted railway carriage.

Address Bitton Railway Station, Bath Road, Bitton, BS30 6HD, +44 (0)117 9325538, www.avonvalleyrailway.org // Getting there Cycle via the Bristol & Bath Railway Path, or take bus 37 or 43 to Bitton // Hours Apr–Sep regular Sat & Sun services & Wed in school holidays; check website for timetables and special events // Ages 2+

TIP: Cherry Gardens play area is located near the car park.

6_ BE WEIRD, BE WILD, BE WONDERFUL

A playhub where you can be whoever you want to be!

A two-year-old doctor weighs a pumpkin on some scales in the middle of a sandpit. Nearby, a six-month-old boy bashes the keys on a typewriter before deciding that eating them with his one tooth is more fun. At the other end of a fancy dress rail, an old-fashioned rotary dial telephone is picked up. 'Hello, is that mummy?' the caller shouts into the earpiece, as her mother takes photos on her mobile.

As well as having a brilliant name, Be Weird, Be Wild, Be Wonderful, is a brilliant place for playing. 'We encourage you to come along and share in our love of play,' says its website. 'There's authentic and natural open-ended resources that encourage curiosity with creative and imaginative play, with resources and space for babies and toddlers to explore and discover.' This is one way of saying that play is at the heart of everything happening here, with 90-minute play sessions happening several times each day, as well as regular events such as SEND support sessions, and twin and triplet meet-ups.

In what was once a Morrisons supermarket, discover a smorgasbord of sensory play potentials. Be tempted by the iced rings and Bourbon biscuits in the glass jars, and don't miss the artificial grass area outside with its tunnels to crawl through. On the way outside you will also find a few books to read in a Bedouin-style tent, if everything else isn't too much of a distraction.

Address 129–133 Bath Road, Longwell Green, BS30 9DD, www.beweirdbewildbewonderful.com // Getting there Bus 44 or 45, cycle racks outside // Hours Mon–Fri everyday play slots 10.30am–noon, 12.30–2pm & 2.30–4pm, Sat 10am–noon // Ages Under-5s

TIP: Aspects Leisure Park in Longwell Green has a bowling alley and multiplex cinema.

7_ BEAR WITH ME

A mysterious sculpture with a comforting message

In a nook within a flight of stairs overlooking a busy road, a teddy bear tenderly puts a paw on the shoulders of a person wearing a hoody who is holding their head in their hands. This mysterious sculpture by an anonymous artist appeared overnight in 2020, and was quickly taken to heart by people across Bristol because of its comforting message on what was World Suicide Prevention Day.

Comfort can come in all shapes and sizes, and for the artist behind the piece, Getting Up To Stuff, this particular sculpture was a 're-minder of how, as children, we turn for comfort to our soft toys when the world is shouting in our face. Sadly, for so many men that option is removed as they grow up and no alternative takes its place.'

Getting Up To Stuff's work often appears in meaning-ful locations. One sculpture can still be found next to a former toilet block on the Downs in memory of toi-let attendant Victoria Hughes, who looked after many women. Another of his sculptures was placed outside the Bag of Nails a few hundred yards down Jacob's Wells Road from Bear With Me, this time a cat as a nod to the famous 'cat pub'.

Speaking to the Bristol 24/7 Behind the Headlines podcast, Get-ting Up To Stuff said that he is a 'disobedient artist' who puts his work around Bristol for his own 'nefarious purposes', creating art about 'whatever the subject de-mands and the location al-lows'. He added: 'I'm not a street artist, I'm not an installation artist, I don't know what I am really. I'm just a bloke that does stuff.'

TIP: Jacob's Wells Theatre on what is now Brandon House on Jacob's Wells Road was Bristol's first purpose-built playhouse, operating from 1729 to 1799.

8_BLAISE CASTLE

The nearest Bristol has to a castle

Unlike Castle Park in the centre of Bristol, Blaise Castle really does have a castle. Okay, it's not really a castle, but it does have four turrets and battlements. It might not have a moat or a drawbridge, but it's the nearest that Bristol has to a castle, so it'll have to do.

But if it looks like a castle and is called a castle, why is it not a castle? Built on the highest part of the Blaise Castle Estate where there once stood a hill fort in Roman times and later chapels to St Werburgh and after that St Blaise, this castle is in fact a folly: what that means is that it is a building – often a small 'castle' or 'temple' – that has been built as a decoration in a large garden or park. This folly was commissioned by wealthy Bristol merchant Thomas Farr in 1766 as a summerhouse that he could show off to his friends, and originally had two fully furnished floors.

If you time your trip to Blaise for when volunteers open up the castle for visitors on some summer Sundays (look out for the flag flying), climb the steps to the roof to get a fine view from the top. From the top of the castle you can see as far as the Cotswolds and the Mendips, or imagine that you are defending your position from an attacking army!

Just one question remains: who was Blaise? St Blaise was the Bishop of Sebastea in Armenia around 1,700 years ago, and is best known for healing the sick. Even animals would come to him to be cured. He is the patron saint of wool combers, wild animals, candle makers and ailments of the throat.

Address Blaise Castle Estate, Kings Weston Road, Henbury, BS10 7QS, +44 (0)117 9222000, www.bristol.gov.uk/museums-parks-sports-culture/blaise-castle-estate // Getting there Bus 1, 2, 3, 4, 76, 623 and MC5 all stop nearby // Hours Daily 7.30am, with various closing times depending on the season; see website for details // Ages 3+

TIP: Blaise Castle Estate has one of the biggest play parks in Bristol.

9_ BOTANIC GARDEN

500 million years of plant evolution

In the whole world, there is only one spot where the Bristol whitebeam, Bristol onion and Bristol rock-cress grow in the wild. Yes, Bristol! To be more specific, the Avon Gorge (see ch. 45) where unique conditions have led to these plants' evolutions. If you can't make it to the gorge, head nearby to the other side of the Downs from Clifton where, on a small rocky outcrop at the University of Bristol Botanic Garden, you can find the plants without the need for any mountaineering.

The botanic garden's logo features the leaves of the whitebeam, but it's just one of hundreds of plants, trees and flowers here. Collect information sheets from the welcome lodge to help you on a hunt. Find water lilies, some of the first flowers to appear on Earth, whose spongy seeds float away and then sink to the bottom of the pond to grow new plants. Hovering above might be colourful dragonflies. You might even spot a kestrel or sparrowhawk soaring even higher as you make your way along paths made of bark, gravel or stones guiding you through the site.

Make sure you take the path to the glasshouses, where you will find plants with leaves as big as you. You won't need to leave here to find flora from as far away as the Amazon and the Azores. By the end of your visit, you will be a bona fide botanist. See if you can discover what plants need to help them grow, recognise different parts of the plant, find out the role of seeds, and why there are different plants in distinct environments – including here in Bristol.

Address Stoke Park Road, Stoke Bishop, BS9 1JG, +44 (0)117 4282041, www.botanic-garden.bristol.ac.uk // Getting there Bus 4, get off at the top of Stoke Hill; bus 1 or 2, get off at White Tree Roundabout and walk along Saville Road to Stoke Hill; plenty of bike racks // Hours Daily 10am–4.30pm // Ages 3+

TIP: Get cakes in the on-site Chandos Deli café.

10 _ BRANDON HILL WATERFALLS

Spring into action

Walk close to the top of Brandon Hill and listen out for the sounds of gurgling and burbling. No, not a new-born baby being taken out for a stroll in their buggy but a water feature perfect for exploring. Budding civil engineers will love to help (or hinder!) the water on its way down to the larger pools at the bottom. Find a strong stick to move the gathered detritus of leaves and moss out of the way, or use then to dam up the channels.

Unlike water, humans can head uphill. Follow one of the streams nearest the Edward VII oak (see ch. 35), the path crossing over the route of the water with the help of a large stepping stone. Water flows down a series of nine small pools, the top one of which is fed by water cascading down a rocky bank. The bravest young explorers can veer off the main path to attempt to find the source.

The other channel usually flows with greater velocity and volume from almost directly below Cabot Tower. A small bridge over the stream midway down its course is a great photo opportunity. The large pool a few feet beneath the bridge can sometimes appear like an oil slick, but look closer and it is in fact frogspawn. A large flat(ish) boulder in the water is just close enough for jumping on – and the water is not deep if you fall in!

Between two of the channels, look out for a brass plaque on the ground, put here in 2010 by Bristol Food For Free. It's a map of Brandon Hill featuring a whole array of wild fruits. Who needs to bring a picnic to the park?

Address Brandon Hill, BS1 5RR, www.bristol.gov.uk/museums-parks-sports-culture/brandon-hill // Getting there 5-minute walk from Park Street // Hours Accessible 24 hours // Ages 3+

TIP: At the bottom of Brandon Hill is a playground featuring a sandy area for little ones.

11_BRIDGE SWINGS

Keeping the harbour shipshape

There has long been a rumour that Plimsoll Bridge rotates on a bed of mercury. It's a good story, but one that's sadly not true. Measuring 269 feet long and weighing in at 865 tonnes, the bridge's giant bulk actually rotates on ball bearings. And when it gets stuck, there is always chaos on the roads. Just a few hours after its opening ceremony in 1965, it got stuck for the first time, causing what was then Bristol's biggest ever traffic jam.

Plimsoll Bridge is one of three swing bridges criss-crossing the Floating Harbour, alongside the nearby North Junction Lock Bridge between pubs the Nova Scotia and the Pump House (which once contained the steam engines that generated hydraulic water pressure to make this bridge swing); and Prince Street Bridge between the Arnolfini and M Shed museum (with the Crêpe Cabin in what used to be the bridge operator's booth). This trio need to swing in order to let taller boats pass through, and the bridge swings are always a sight to behold, with Bristolians accustomed to waiting patiently whether on foot, on two wheels or on four.

> TIP: Find 'Brunel's Other Bridge' underneath Plimsoll Bridge.

Along the New Cut, Ashton Avenue Bridge and Vauxhall Bridge also used to swing but have not done so for many years as boats rarely travel along this section of water, which remains tidal to allow the Floating Harbour to remain at a constant level. Fans of bridges might be keen to note that Ashton Avenue Bridge used to be a double-decker swing bridge, the upper level being a road and the lower level carrying a freight-only railway branch line that closed in 1987.

Address Various locations // Hours
Accessible 24 hours // Ages 3+

12_ BRISTOL AQUARIUM

It's better down where it's wetter

From the docks to the Avon, Bristol is a city built on water. The odd family of otters has been spied in the city and a seal has even got as far as Hanham, but to see undersea creatures from across the world, you need to head to Bristol Aquarium to imagine you're in *The Little Mermaid* or *Finding Nemo*.

Talking of *Finding Nemo*, can you find the orange and white clownfish, or blue and yellow regal tang? The latter is better known as the absent-minded Dory in the Disney films, but you're not likely to forget some of its neighbours here in a hurry. There are red-bellied piranhas whose fearsome reputation precedes them, stingrays that cut through the water like gliders, and fish as small as a fingernail or as big as you.

Try to time your visit with a feeding session. You might get splashed in the excitement! Viewing areas allow some fish to swim over your head and you can even measure yourself to see if you are the same size as a lobster, an eel or even a shark. How do you measure up to the giant Pacific octopus? With three hearts and bright blue blood, individuals living in aquariums are known to have sneaked out at night to raid nearby fish-filled displays.

You might think that this attraction is just for fish and other aquatic creatures, but it also has its own 'urban jungle'. Walk from a shipwreck into this botanical house, where exotic plants try to escape the temperature-controlled tropical paradise through the windows to the outside world, as if to spite the fish whose fates are sealed inside.

Address Anchor Square, Anchor Road, BS1 5TT, +44 (0)117 9298929, www.bristolaquarium.co.uk // **Getting there** Short walk from Millennium Square // **Hours** Daily 10am–6pm // **Ages** 4+

TIP: Look out for occasional film screenings in the former IMAX cinema that is part of the aquarium.

13_ BRISTOL CASTLE

Once England's largest Norman castle

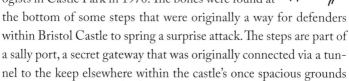

The skeleton of a monkey was uncovered by archaeologists in Castle Park in 1970. The bones were found at the bottom of some steps that were originally a way for defenders within Bristol Castle to spring a surprise attack. The steps are part of a sally port, a secret gateway that was originally connected via a tunnel to the keep elsewhere within the castle's once spacious grounds in what is today Castle Park. Despite the walls of the keep being around 25 feet thick, now only a few fragments of the once mighty fortress remain.

The ruins of the keep can be found in one corner of the park, having later been incorporated within a Victorian ironworks. The castle held an enviable defensive position, and arrow slits within a wall once overlooking the original course of the River Avon can still be found beside the small path next to the water source heat pump that was built in 2022.

Castle Ditch Bridge spans the last visible part of the castle's moat, which still flows underneath some nearby roads and buildings before joining up with a section of the underground River Frome near the Harvey Nichols store. Find the best view of the moat and its disappearing act from a footpath accessed off Queen Street.

> **TIP:** St Edith's Well in Castle Park was one of Bristol's original sources of fresh water.

Everything we have discovered so far of the castle has been underground. But there is one remarkably intact surviving fragment of it above ground in what is now the council-owned Vaulted Chambers Café. The clue is in the name: the café is thought to have originally been the entrance to the castle's great hall. Walk into the Vaulted Chambers and step back in time almost 1000 years.

Address Castle Park, BS2 0HQ // Getting there 5-minute walk from Cabot Circus // Hours Accessible 24 hours // Ages 3+

14_BRISTOL FERRY BOATS

Give them a wave!

The blue and yellow ferry boats going back and forth along the water are an iconic sight of Bristol. Bristol Ferry Boats are the vessels with the distinctive blue and yellow livery, but look out too for Number Seven boats whose prows are painted with sharks' teeth, and Bristol Packet who give regular tours around the Floating Harbour during the summer season.

Ah

The best place to jump on the ferry boats is at the Cascade Steps close to Watershed, where there are often two ferries waiting: one to go under Pero's Bridge (see ch. 75) and turn left towards Temple Meads; the other to turn right towards Underfall Yard (see ch. 68). Go one way or take a round trip, waving to hail the ferry from a stop. Once you're on board, it's almost the law to wave at landlubbers, who will usually wave back! You get some of the best views of Bristol from these boats, which also have regular return trips to Beese's tea gardens an hour's sail along the River Avon.

The ferry boats may now be a familiar sight, but they and the whole harbour came close to not being here. The docks closed to industry in 1969, and some people in the council thought that the best thing to do would be to build a large new road network in its place. But there was widespread consternation with the forerunner of the annual Harbour Festival taking place in 1971 to show that the city's inland waterways were perfect for people to enjoy. Fortunately, the plans to concrete over the harbour were scrapped and the water is today a place for leisure not lorries.

Oh

Address There are more than a dozen ferry stops, +44 (0)117 9273416, www.bristolferry.com (map of ferry stops and the full timetable are available on the website) // Getting there Cascade Steps is located a short walk from fountains // Hours Ferries run 10am–5pm daily // Ages 2+

TIP: Cascade Steps make a fun place to play on a hot day.

15__ BUMPSY

Move over Banksy!

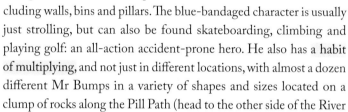

Move over Banksy, Bumpsy is in town! And he is prolific. Find Mr Bump on locations including walls, bins and pillars. The blue-bandaged character is usually just strolling, but can also be found skateboarding, climbing and playing golf: an all-action accident-prone hero. He also has a habit of multiplying, and not just in different locations, with almost a dozen different Mr Bumps in a variety of shapes and sizes located on a clump of rocks along the Pill Path (head to the other side of the River Avon from the Portway and follow the path underneath the Clifton Suspension Bridge).

Portraits of the famous Roger Hargreaves figure first started popping up around Sea Mills close to the Avon and Trym rivers in 2021. The anonymous artist was soon dubbed Bumpsy, and began adding this tag to their pieces. But not everyone sees the works as a ray of Little Miss Sunshine. Instead, there have been Mr Angry reactions as Bumpsy has painted on information signs and heritage walls, including near the listed Kingsweston iron bridge.

Since Bumpsy's artworks first appeared, Luke Merrett has attempted to locate each and every one of them. As this guidebook was going to the printers in 2023, Luke had mapped and taken photos of 40 Mr Bumps, as well as creating a 20-mile trail if you want to track them all down yourself. (Find the map at leave-the-road-and.run/mr-bumps-friday-route-recommendation.) New pieces are still popping up all the time, with the identity of the mysterious Bumpsy – like Banksy – a closely guarded secret.

Address Various locations particularly around Sea Mills, Blaise and Kingsweston, www.instagram.com/mr_bumpsy // **Hours** Accessible 24 hours // **Ages 2+**

TIP: Find Banksy's Mild Mild West on Stokes Croft and Hanging Man at the bottom of Park Street.

16_ BURGERS ON A BOAT

Mouth-watering food on the water

Bristol is a city built on waterways. So where better to have lunch than sitting above the glistening waves? Not just anywhere in the city either, but close to Bristol Bridge, where the original Saxon settlement of Bristol grew up around and which gave the place its name. Bristol was founded in Saxon times where the rivers Avon and Frome once met. A wooden bridge was built across the Avon, and the settlement was known as Brigstow, meaning 'the place at the bridge'. The local dialect caused an 'l' to be added to the end of this, and over time the name became Bristol.

But back to burgers and, more specifically, Three Brothers Burgers on Welsh Back, which may specialise in burgers but isn't actually owned by three brothers. Instead, it is named after the three masts on the boat that used to be called the *Spyglass*, after the famous pub in *Treasure Island* (see ch. 95).

The burgers here are all made in-house using locally reared, grass-fed, longhorn beef, served in a soft glazed brioche bun with their own dressing, baby gem lettuce and red onion. Three Brothers now have almost as many veggie and vegan options as the meat variety, with their succulent plant-based patty not only vegan but also gluten-free. All of their vegan burgers can be made more delicious by adding vegan cheese, vegan dressing and a vegan bun, with extras including vegan bacon.

Get a classic burger – either meat or veggie – with fries for just £6 every day until 5pm. It's one of the best value food deals in Bristol.

Address Three Brothers, Welsh Back, BS1 4SB, +44 (0)117 9277050, www.threebrothersburgers.co.uk // Getting there Short walk from Queen Square or from Bristol Bridge // Hours Mon–Wed noon–9pm, Thu–Sat noon–10pm, Sun noon–6pm // Ages 4+

TIP: Grain Barge and Under the Stars are also boats you can eat and drink on.

17_CABOT TOWER

Go on an explore to the top

Christopher who? Ask a Bristolian who discovered North America and the answer may surprise you. In Bristol, we have a heroic explorer adopted as our own: Giovanni Caboto, better known as John Cabot. Read one of (count 'em) three plaques around the base of the Cabot Tower, which was built at the top of Brandon Hill between 1897 and 1898.

'This tower was erected by public subscription in the 61st year of the reign of Queen Victoria to commemorate the fourth centenary of the discovery of the continent of North America on the 24th June 1497 by John Cabot who sailed from this port in the Bristol ship *Matthew* with a Bristol crew under letters patent granted by King Henry VII to that navigator and his sons Lewis, Sebastian and Sanctus.'

So there we have it: it must be official because it's on a plaque. What Cabot 'discovered' was Newfoundland (the clue is in the name), or it could have been Labrador or perhaps Cape Breton Island. Somewhere in modern-day Canada anyway. After going ashore, Cabot and his crew saw signs indicating that the area was inhabited, but they saw no people so they took possession of the land for the English King. A 15th-century version of finders keepers.

TIP: Boston Tea Party on Park Street serves breakfast and brunch all day.

Climb the spiral staircase of the Cabot Tower and be prepared to squeeze past fellow explorers going the other way. From the surprisingly spacious viewing platform at the top, the best views are looking south with a panorama taking in the colourful suburbs of Totterdown and beyond to where the city turns into the countryside.

Address Brandon Hill, BS1 5RR, +44 (0)117 9222200, www.bristol.gov.uk/museums-parks-sports-culture/brandon-hill // Getting there 5-minute walk from Park Street // Hours Daily from 8am, closing times vary so check website // Ages 4+

18_ CAMERA OBSCURA

A photographic pioneer

When you take photos of the Clifton Suspension Bridge (see ch. 28) from Observatory Hill – also one of the best places in Bristol to watch hot air balloons during the annual Balloon Fiesta – you will  be close to an early method of capturing light; the concepts and science behind which eventually led to the cameras we use today.

Bristol's Camera Obscura is on the top floor of the Clifton Observatory, which was once a windmill used to grind corn for the poor. Its latest incarnation as an observatory originally saw a telescope installed on the roof by artist William West, which he replaced in 1829 with the camera obscura. Choose as bright a day as possible to visit to see an image of the surrounding area projected onto a circular white dish in a darkened room. It's like watching a live video of crystal clear clarity. You can even use a white piece of paper to 'pick up' people as they walk by.

Like having the remote control at home, take hold of the wooden lever and slowly turn it in a circular direction to control the lens and mirror on the roof of the building that then projects a bird's eye perspective in real-time onto the white dish.

Within the Clifton Observatory are also rooms with displays including some of the earliest surviving photographs of Bristol. There is also the 360 Café with a rooftop terrace that is among the most sought-after spots in the city, where you can enjoy an indulgent hot chocolate. And remember to visit the Giant's Cave (see ch. 45), accessed via the same entrance, but heading down rather than up.

Address Clifton Observatory, Litfield Place, Clifton, BS8 3LT, +44 (0)117 9741242, www.cliftonobservatory.com // Getting there 4-minute walk from Clifton Suspension Bridge // Hours Apr–Oct daily 10am–5pm, Nov–Mar 10am–4pm // Ages 4+

TIP: The earth ramparts of an Iron Age hill fort can still be found under the trees at the wooded edges of Observatory Hill.

19_CASTLE PARK TREE TRAIL

A green lung in the city centre

While in leafy Castle Park, take some time to imagine what was here before this park was created in the 1970s. It might be empty of buildings today, but this was the historic centre of Bristol where some roads were once so narrow that neighbours on either side could almost shake hands with each other out of their upstairs windows. On the site of the original castle, the area grew into a thriving neighbourhood that was all but destroyed during the Blitz of 1940.

So, on what were homes, shops and even a hospital, is now Castle Park, which contains more than 300 trees, and is a popular green lung in the city centre. The best way to explore all of these trees is by following the Castle Park Tree Trail, which helpfully includes leaf illustrations. On the 1,000-yard-long mostly step-free trail, look out for special trees including the strawberry tree, whose small white flowers appear in the autumn at the same time as large strawberry-like fruit, the Judas tree, whose bright pink flowers grow right on its twigs and branches, and the cherry trees along 'cherry avenue'.

There are plenty of other things to look out for while in Castle Park. There are the ruins of two bombed-out churches, water fountains, a garden commemorating Sikh soldiers, and the Normandy Garden of Peace. The area around St Peter's Church is a popular place for parkour, and below this is a plaque surrounded by colourful mosaics to remember the four Bristol men who died fighting on the Republican side in the Spanish Civil War.

TIP: The winding Castle Bridge connects Castle Park to Finzels Reach.

Address Castle Park, BS1 3XB, www.bristolcivicsociety.org.uk/castle-park-tree-trail // Getting there 3-minute walk from St Nick's Market // Hours Accessible 24 hours // Ages 4+

20_CHANCE & COUNTERS

Never a risk of being bored

You've probably heard of *Bananagrams* and *Buckaroo*, dabbled in *Dobble*, mastered *Monopoly* and trialled *Trivial Pursuit*. But have you clocked *Clock It*, gone cuckoo at *Go Cuckoo* or practised *Piratissimo*? And then there are *Here, Kitty, Kitty!*, *Hey, That's My Fish!* and *Rhino Hero*, *Taco Cat Goat Cheese Pizza*, *Ticket to Ride* and *Tumble Tree*. Say anything during *Say Anything*, take a sneak peek at *Sneak Peek* and walk the plank with *Walk the Plank*. And go from A to Z, from *Agricola* and *Animal Upon Animal* to *Zitternix* and *Zoowaboo*.

If you haven't realised it by now, there are a lot of board games at Chance & Counters. It's impossible to get bored here with more than 600 games from new re-leases to old-school classics. The café is a purpose-built space for board gamers of all ages and abilities to enjoy. Chance & Counters' first home in Bristol has proved so popular since being opened in 2016 by friends Luke, Steve and Richard that they now have two others in Cardiff and Birmingham, and are currently looking for a bigger home in Bristol.

TIP: RePlay on Cheltenham Road also has dozens of board games and table tennis in its basement.

Don't know what to play? Is the choice just too great? No problem! Just find a gaming guru, who will be able to give you personalised rec-ommendations related to what you love playing. Do you enjoy fearlessly scaling the highest houses looking for burglars and rogues? Try *Rhino Hero*. Or prefer guessing how many animals can fit on a raft? *Zoowa-boo* is for you! Chance & Counters can get busy on evenings and week-ends especially in the school holidays, so advance booking is advised.

Address 20 Christmas Steps, BS1 5BS, +44 (0)117 3291700, www.chanceandcounters.com/bristol // Getting there 5-minute walk from fountains // Hours Sun–Wed 10am–11pm, Thu–Sat 10am–midnight // Ages Children of all ages

21_ THE CHAOTIC PENDULUM

It baffles even the finest mathematical minds

Among the graves, brasses, organ and whale's rib bone reputedly brought back to Bristol from John Cabot's voyage of 'discovery' to North America, there is one part of St Mary Redcliffe far removed from the order and tranquillity of the rest of the church. A church that Queen Elizabeth I no less called 'the fairest, goodliest and most famous parish church in England' during her 1574 visit to Bristol. This is the Chaotic Pendulum, a device that even the finest mathematical minds cannot predict what will do next.

Mounted on a wooden cross are two pendulums, one large and mostly horizontal, the other smaller and mostly vertical. A steady stream of water is fed to the larger pendulum, which water can flow on and off, with the weight of the water and subsequent tipping out of the liquid causing its unpredictable movement.

An information board next to the Chaotic Pendulum explains the scene that greets visitors: 'Water, which is recycled, slowly flows into the centre of the cross beam, which tips to let it out. But which way will it tip? What is remarkable is that with all the science in the world, no one can predict exactly how it will be moving a minute from now. This is the way the world is. In this simple machine, you are looking at a new frontier in our understanding of the world. Scientists call it chaos. Some people look to science for certainties on which to base their lives. Increasingly we realise our knowledge can never provide certainty, even for this simple machine. The world is a more wonderful and a more surprising place than we could have imagined.'

Address St Mary Redcliffe, Colston Parade, Redcliffe, BS1 6RA, +44 (0)330 1594919, www.stmaryredcliffe.co.uk // Getting there 5-minute walk from Temple Meads, 5-minute walk from Queen Square // Hours Mon–Sat 8am–5pm, Sun noon–4.30pm // Ages 4+

TIP: Bump Rollerdisco
regularly comes
to Redcliffe Wharf.

22_ CHEER ON BRISTOL BEARS

C'mon Bris!

Under the inspirational leadership of director of rugby Pat Lam, Bristol Bears have been one of the city's best sporting success stories of recent years. If you're a fan of the oval ball, or even if you're not, watching the Bears is an excellent afternoon or evening out, especially if they win.

A matchday experience at Ashton Gate is far more than the 80 minutes on the pitch. There is live music before kick-off and after the final whistle, some of Bristol's best pies to eat courtesy of Buxton & Bird, and sausage sandwiches from Pigsty, co-owned by former Bristol player Olly Kohn. Watch the players come onto the pitch accompanied by a few pyrotechnics, celebrate the tries, join in the fun with stadium announcer Ian Downs and pose for photos with players or mascot Briz at full-time. Get your own bobble hat or any item of branded paraphernalia from the stadium shop, where a player is often available to sign merchandise before a game.

It's not just about the men of course, with Bristol Bears Women playing their rugby at Shaftsbury Park. And are you a Robin or a Gashead? If football is more your thing, like the Bears, Bristol City men also play at Ashton Gate, with City Women playing at the Robins High Performance Centre in Failand. North of the river, Bristol Rovers play at the Memorial Stadium while Bristol Rovers Women's – an award-winning initiative of Bristol Rovers Community Trust – play at Lockleaze Sports Centre, which is also where Bristol's first padel courts (see ch. 77) are located.

Address Ashton Gate Stadium, Ashton, BS3 2EJ, + 44 (0)117 9630600, www.ashtongatestadium.co.uk // Getting there 30-minute walk from harbourside; lots of bike parking on site; 15-minute walk from Parson Street station; close to bus routes 24 and M2 // Hours Dependent on fixtures so check website for details // Ages 6+

TIP: RugbyTots is a great introduction to rugby for children from age 2+.

23_ CHEZ MARCEL

What's your flavour?

'Hello, bonjour, ça va?' Walk into Chez Marcel and be greeted warmly by owner Greg Raccommandato. Back in his native France, Greg used to own a crêperie, and he has recreated the traditional formula the other side of the English Channel. Named after his son, Chez Marcel is a delicious and authentic taste of the national dish of Brittany.

Chez Marcel specialises in two things and does both very well indeed: *galettes de sarrasin* or buckwheat galettes, and *crêpes au froment* or wheat pancakes. So you can have a savoury pancake for your main course and a sweet pancake for dessert. All the food here is prepared daily, made out of only a handful of fresh ingredients and cooked on a hot girdle. Once the galette or crêpe is ready, Greg and his team fold in the sides to create an envelope over the fillings.

For the galette, these fillings can be everything from the traditional ham and Emmental cheese to choices including *La Nordique*: smoked salmon, cottage cheese and chives; or *La Saucisse Fumée*: smoked sau-

sage and Emmental cheese. Vegans no longer miss out here either, with vegan cheese available.

Pancake purists will choose the lighter crêpe with just fresh lemon and sugar. But be sure to experiment with more adventurous options including the house favourite *La Marcel*: Nutella, nuts and Chantilly (whipped cream); or *La Mont Blanc*: chestnut cream, vanilla ice cream and Chantilly. If you want to add a bit of excitement, get a grown-up to order a flambée crêpe, which Greg or one of his enthusiastic members of staff will set alight at your table.

TIP: Walk through the alleyway next to Chez Marcel to find the historic Tailors Court.

Address 43 Broad Street,
BS1 2EP, +44 (0)7947 955656,
www.chezmarcelcreperie.com //
Getting there Short walk from
St Nick's Market // Hours
Tue–Sun 9am–4pm // Ages 3+

24_ CHILDREN'S SCRAPSTORE

A cave of wonders for creatives

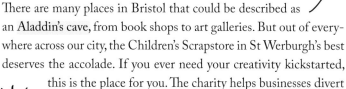

There are many places in Bristol that could be described as an **Aladdin's cave**, from book shops to art galleries. But out of everywhere across our city, the Children's Scrapstore in St Werburgh's best deserves the accolade. If you ever need your creativity kickstarted, this is the place for you. The charity helps businesses divert reusable waste away from landfill, and at the same time helps improve art and play opportunities for children.

One of their mottos is '**making waste things play things**' and a look at some recent items of scrap shows just why this is an Aladdin's cave. There may not be a genie in a bottle, but there are (or were) – deep breath – plastic cones, coffee sacks, assorted buttons, cardboard tubes, rubber bands, squirty bottle caps, Braille paper, bra straps and so much more. What would you make from all of that?

An art shop on site has a few more traditional art and craft items for sale. Don't mind getting dirty? Children's Scrapstore runs **messy play sessions** for under-fives every week, and has sessions for older and younger children in the school holidays, including stay and play and drop-off sessions, with themes including animation, scrap costumes and space adventure.

Children's Scrapstore started in 1982 from a small garage, and has arrived in St Werburgh's via Brislington and Welsh Back as well as a while spent in the Cameron Balloons hot air balloon factory in Bedminster. They now divert around 200 tonnes from landfill each year, thanks to their focus on **reuse, play and art**.

TIP: Better Food almost next door is the original shop of a successful Bristol business selling organic groceries and fresh produce, and also includes a café.

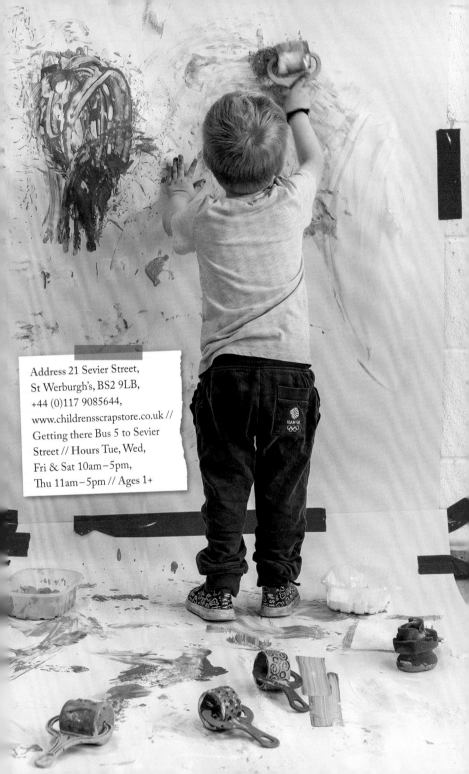

Address 21 Sevier Street,
St Werburgh's, BS2 9LB,
+44 (0)117 9085644,
www.childrensscrapstore.co.uk //
Getting there Bus 5 to Sevier
Street // Hours Tue, Wed,
Fri & Sat 10am−5pm,
Thu 11am−5pm // Ages 1+

25_ CIRCOMEDIA

Run away and join the circus

When Little Amal, a giant puppet of a young Syrian refugee, walked through Bristol in June 2022, she was welcomed on Corn Street by performers from Circomedia. There, she watched transfixed as acrobats, unicyclists and jugglers – and sometimes a combination of all three – created a party atmosphere. The performers were from Circomedia's Youth Circus, where children aged from two to 18 have the chance to enter the extraordinary world of contemporary circus and physical theatre.

After-school sessions give children a huge range of new skills and the confidence to perform them. From tightrope to trapeze, you'll soon be performing tricks that you never thought possible. Classes in Bristol take place at the former St Paul's Church on Portland Square in St Paul's, whose high ceilings are a perfect space for circus. It's also where annual showcases happen, where you can wow the adults with your newly acquired expertise.

For the littlest circus performers, Sundays at Portland Square are pre-school classes where parents can walk the tight wire, juggle scarves and swing on the trapeze with their children. Like when Little Amal came to visit, there are regular opportunities to perform, for those who want to, at events throughout the year, including the Harbour Festival and St Paul's Carnival. And if one day a week is not enough, youth camps run during the school holidays at Circomedia's Kingswood base. At Circomedia, you can run away and join the circus without even leaving Bristol.

Address Portland Square, St Paul's, BS2 8SJ, +44 (0)117 9247615, www.circomedia.com/youth-circus // Getting there 3-minute walk from Cabot Circus // Hours Check website for details of classes and shows // Ages 2+

TIP: Artist Residence hotel on Portland Square has a number of family-friendly rooms.

26_CITY OF BRISTOL GYMNASTICS CENTRE

From toddlers to international standard athletes

Don't be alarmed when you see tumbling tigers and leaping leopards take to the floor of the City of Bristol Gymnastics Centre. These are the names of the classes for two- to three-year-olds and over-threes as they take their first tumbles and leaps to become fully fledged young gymnasts. There are plenty of other classes here for children of all ages, and not just in gymnastics, with parkour a popular activity – in padded surroundings, contrasting with its usual urban environment.

Tumbling Tigers is a class for both toddlers and their parents, while Leaping Leopards is an independent class for those independent over-threes. Stay and play sessions allow a child and their adult to explore the gym apparatus in their own time. The pre-school sessions are more structured, led by qualified coaches and designed to take the children from free play to a class programme.

City of Bristol Gymnastics Centre was purpose-built to provide the best experience for gymnasts of all levels – from toddlers to international standard athletes. Over in Easton, Hawks Gymnastic Club is another child-friendly club but within a converted Co-Op building. Its most famous gymnast is Claudia Fragapane, who has won multiple world and European medals, competed for Team GB at the Olympics, and taken part in *Strictly Come Dancing* – with fellow Bristolian Jayde Adams taking to the dancefloor in 2022.

> TIP: The Big Hideout is an adventure playground on Teyfant Road.

Address Teyfant Road, Hartcliffe, BS13 0RF, +44 (0)117 3773420, www.bristolgymnastics.co.uk // Getting there Bus 75 to Bishport Avenue // Hours Check website for timetables // Ages 2+

27_THE CLIFTON ARCADE

An early shopping mall

When you're next in a modern shopping centre, you can thank a picturesque collection of indoor shops in Bristol for the ease of having so many places to spend your money under one roof. What is now the Clifton Arcade was an early Victorian version of the shopping mall. But it went very wrong for its financial backer, architect and builder, Joseph King.

After opening in 1878, the 'King's Bazaar and Winter Garden' was unfortunately an instant flop. No businesses wanted the spaces and, instead, the building spent most of the next 100 years as a furniture warehouse. It was only in 1992 that King's grand plans finally came true and at last shops moved in.

Today, you can visit Village, one of those shops where you need nothing they sell but want everything! Try the house special bubble teas at Jo's, including watermelon galaxy and vanilla cotton candy. Look through the windows of Clifton Village Antiques; if you have wandered around the Lanes in Brighton, this jewellery shop will feel familiar. There is also art at Hidden, restored Chinese antique furniture at Nook Deco, a jungle's worth of house plants at Interior Oasis and Heron Books, Bristol's smallest bookshop.

Prior to restoration, the Clifton Arcade featured in a music video for Del Amitri (ask your grandparents!) for their song, 'Nothing Ever Happens', which reached number 11 in the UK singles charts in January 1990. It also featured in several episodes of *Casualty*, the long-running BBC hospital drama that used to be filmed in Bristol.

Address Boyce's Avenue, Clifton, BS8 4AA, +44 (0)117 9744348, www.cliftonarcade.com // Getting there 10-minute walk from Clifton Suspension Bridge; bus 8 to Clifton Village // Hours Mon–Fri 10am–5.30pm, Sat 10am–6pm, Sun 11am–4pm // Ages 4+

TIP: You never know what you will find in the Oxfam shop on Regent Street.

28_ CLIFTON SUSPENSION BRIDGE

Brunel's masterpiece of engineering

On 19 February, 1896, there was only one place in Bristol where juggler George Zanetto could perform his most famous trick: catching on a fork held in his mouth a turnip dropped from a great height. The Clifton Suspension Bridge had been open for less than 30 years when Zanetto drew a crowd of thousands of onlookers to witness his daring feat. A contemporary account in the *Illustrated Police News* said that 'the blow slightly stunned him, though he quickly recovered. What the effect would have been, however, if the turnip had struck him on the head is better left unstated.'

Zanetto has not been the only daredevil to pay a visit to Isambard Kingdom Brunel's masterpiece of engineering. In July 1927, RAF pilot F. G. Wayman flew a Bristol Fighter two-seat biplane under the bridge to win a bet of five shillings. And it was the site of the world's first modern-day bungee jump in 1979 when David Kirke of the Oxford University Dangerous Sports Club jumped off wearing a top hat and holding a glass of champagne.

The bridge may be Bristol's most well-known landmark, but some of its secrets are still being revealed. It was only in 2002 when a complex network of vaulted chambers within the abutment below the Leigh Woods tower was rediscovered by builder Ray Brown, who had been replacing paving around the towers. Until then, it had been assumed that the abutments on both side of the Avon Gorge were solid. Find out all about the bridge in the excellent Visitor Centre on the Leigh Woods side.

Address Bridge Road, Clifton, BS8 3PA, +44 (0)117 9223571, www.cliftonbridge.org.uk // Getting there Bus 8 to Clifton Village, then a 5-minute walk, or X3 to Clifton Lodge entrance of the Ashton Court Estate and a 5-minute walk // Hours Bridge open 365 days a year, Visitor Centre open daily 10am–5pm // Ages 3+

TIP: Get snacks and drinks from Chapter & Holmes in a tuk-tuk on the Leigh Woods side of the bridge.

29_CLIMB ABOARD CONCORDE

Supersonic family fun

If you plot a graph to mark the achievements of human beings since our ancestors first crawled out of the ocean, the line would be heading in an upwards trajectory. We have become bigger, stronger and faster. But hang on. We haven't always got faster. There is one blip on the graph when humankind's progress in the field of aviation soared swiftly upwards but then fell back to the ground with a bump.

Within Aerospace Bristol – a museum dedicated to flight, located on the edge of what used to be Filton Airfield – is Concorde Alpha Foxtrot, the last supersonic passenger jet to be built and the last to fly when it returned to its home city in 2003. This magnificent flying marvel is now kept for evermore in a purpose-built hangar that it will never leave; grounded as a monument to the dreams, daring and engineering audacity of a bygone generation.

Climb aboard to step into an aircraft that was once capable of crossing the Atlantic in under three hours, cruising at 1,320 miles per hour (more than twice the speed of sound) and reaching an altitude of 60,000 feet. Also in Concorde's hangar, watch a projection show on the side of the plane and explore a collection of memorabilia.

Concorde may be the centrepiece but it is by no means the only attraction at Aerospace Bristol, which takes a journey through more than a century of aviation history and the part that Bristol people and businesses have played. There are hundreds of exhibits here from small model aircrafts to helicopters, rockets and even missiles.

Address Aerospace Bristol, Hayes Way, Patchway, BS34 5BZ, +44 (0)117 9315315, www.aerospacebristol.org // Getting there Bus m4 to Hayes Way, or 75 or T2 to Gipsy Patch Lane; alternatively, free car parking on site // Hours Tue–Sun 10am–4.30pm during school term time, daily 10am–4.30pm during school holidays // Ages 4+

TIP: Bristol Arena could soon be built within the former Brabazon hangars near Aerospace Bristol.

30_ CLIP 'N CLIMB

Can you reach the top?

Bristol attracts climbers from across the world, drawn here by the city's astonishing natural landscape and unique geology. There aren't many cities with a feature like the Avon Gorge (over which the Clifton Suspension Bridge spans) so close to the centre. There is even a secret cave in the gorge with a guestbook in it that can only be signed by climbers who reach it.

But these expert climbers need to start somewhere, and Clip 'n Climb is an ideal launch pad. The clue is in the name: clip on and then climb up. Each climber wears a harness attached to a rope that almost acts like a reverse bungee cord, helping the climber defy gravity while ascending, and then slowly easing them back down with the help of a special contraption called an auto-belay if they miss a handhold or make it to the top and need to descend.

TIP: If you like Clip 'n Climb, also check out Crazy Climb at Redpoint in Bedminster.

Clip 'n Climb has more than a dozen colourful walls to choose from, which can only be climbed by one person at a time. They are all different: from a New York-style skyscraper to what looks like a giant slice of holey cheese. There are various ways to get up each one if you want to add an extra challenge, and for an extra bonus challenge there is the 'leap of faith' when you climb up a ladder and jump out across the void to grab a hanging bag.

If the challenges of Clip 'n Climb are beginning to feel a bit too tame for you, children from age six can learn to boulder at Bloc next door. Bouldering is climbing without ropes or harnesses and this is a perfect first experience of indoor climbing.

Address Bloc, Units 2–3,
New Gatton Road,
St Werburgh's, BS2 9SH,
+44 (0)117 9558508,
www.blocclimbing.co.uk/
clip-n-climb // Getting
there Bus 5 to James
Street // Hours Mon–Fri
9am–5.30pm, Sat & Sun
9am–6pm // Ages 4+

31_COLSTON'S EMPTY PLINTH

No longer commemorating a slave trader

During a Black Lives Matter march on 7 June, 2020, the statue of Edward Colston was pulled from its plinth by protesters and rolled into the docks. The plinth on which the statue had stood for 125 years remains empty as the city grapples with the decision of how to remember Colston, with the plaque on one side still proclaiming that he was 'one of the most virtuous and wise sons' of Bristol. Colston may have given away much of his huge wealth to charitable causes in the city, but he made his fortune as a leading member of the Royal African Company, which had the British monopoly on the transatlantic slave trade, now also known as the transatlantic trafficking of enslaved Africans.

POWER

In 2022, four people on trial for criminal damage to the statue following its toppling and rolling into the harbour were found not guilty at Bristol Crown Court. Barristers for the 'Colston 4' argued that the statue was 'offensive' and a 'racist hate crime', and that its pulling down came in the wake of decades of campaigning for its removal.

Following the statue's dramatic toppling, many organisations across Bristol began a process of removing Colston's name. So what would you like to see on the empty plinth? The statue itself is likely to go on permanent display at the M Shed (see ch. 62) following a temporary exhibition held there in 2021, with the empty plinth possibly getting a changing series of artworks, and a second plaque explaining Colston's involvement in buying and selling thousands of men, women and children.

TIP: Formerly known as Colston Hall, the Bristol Beacon hosts the annual Hoo-Ha! Festival for children.

Address Colston
Avenue, BS1 4TB //
Getting there 3-minute
walk from fountains //
Hours Accessible
24 hours // Ages 4+

32__DEER HERD

Deer oh deer oh deer

Red, fallow and wild roe deer roam freely within their spacious enclosures among the rolling fields and woods of Ashton Court. Why go all the way to the Scottish Highlands when you can see these majestic creatures just a few miles away from Bristol city centre? Okay, we don't have lochs, mountains or haggis, but for hundreds of years these deer have been resident here, where they are as much at home as hot air balloons.

Ashton Court became a deer park more than 600 years ago. As you can probably imagine, the animals weren't just kept here to be admired, but were hunted for centuries until the estate fell into disrepair after World War II, and the animals took their chance and escaped! In 1959, the land was purchased by Bristol City Council and deer reintroduced a decade later.

Whether arriving into Ashton Court either up the hill from UWE Bristol's Bower Ashton campus or down the hill from the top entrance near the Suspension Bridge, it's always a very special sight when spotting the deer, sometimes just the other side of a fence and other times in the distance well away from human interference.

There is a herd of about a hundred red deer in one area near the mansion house and about the same number of fallow deer on the other side of the estate. Free from hunting and from predators, and with their diets supplemented with hay and sugar-beet, the deer here are bigger than those in the wild. One obvious sign of this is the males' sizeable antlers; you certainly wouldn't want to meet them in a fight.

Address Ashton Court Estate, Long Ashton, BS41 9JN, +44 (0)117 9633438, www.bristol.gov.uk/museums-parks-sports-culture/ashton-court-estate // Getting there 5-minute walk from Clifton Suspension Bridge // Hours Estate open daily from 8am, but closing times are different throughout the year (see website) // Ages 4+

TIP: Deer are occasionally spotted roaming residential streets and even the city centre!

33_EASTON LEISURE CENTRE

Fly down the flume

There's a tantalising glimpse of the water slide at Easton Leisure Centre for anybody travelling along Stapleton Road. There it is! In a shade of blue not dissimilar to the colour of the Caribbean Sea but just in east Bristol. Appearing high up on the side of the building above its car park, turning two tight corners held up by three tall poles before disappearing back inside the building.

When you get inside the building yourself, you need to make your way to the swimming pool to find the rest of the slide. You'll spot the steps up to the start of the slide in one corner of the room, above a pool that you'll soon come cascading into from above. Climb the steps, reach the top, prepare yourself for launch, wait for the green light, and go, go, go!

All under-fives can swim for free here at Easton Leisure Centre, with children aged from four months able to take part in weekly sessions with their adults. These feature an introduction to water movement through songs and games, with children aged from 19 months to three years getting lessons aiming to prepare them for independent swimming. Women-only sessions also take place in the pool, which has a shallow area perfect for the littlest of water babies to splash about safely.

TIP: Find food from across the world on Stapleton Road.

The flume may be the best bit of Easton Leisure Centre but there are plenty more other activities to also enjoy here, with children able to play badminton, basketball, five-a-side football and squash as well as swimming and, of course, climbing up the steps to the water slide.

Address Thrissell Street, Easton, BS5 0SW, +44 (0)117 9558840, www.everyoneactive.com/centre/Easton-Leisure-Centre // Getting there Bus 49 to Stapleton Road // Hours Mon–Fri 6.30am–10.30pm, Sat 7.30am–8pm, Sun 7.30am–9pm // Ages 4 months+

34__ECLECTIC GIFT SHOP

A perfect place for Bristol souvenirs

Imagine painting an intricate scene of Bristol, perhaps of the Clifton Suspension Bridge (see ch. 28) or the SS *Great Britain* (see ch. 46). Maybe you will choose to incorporate the colourful houses of Cliftonwood, and if it's Christmas coming up, add a sprinkling of snow. Now imagine painting your scene, which of course will include a few hot air balloons – this is Bristol after all – with a hook within a glass bauble from the inside. This is a traditional artisan method dating back hundreds of years, and you can see some of the wonderful work at the proudly independent Eclectic Gift Shop in Hanham.

The baubles are painted by Horfield-based artist Rebecca Walker, who is just one of more than 100 people whose products are stocked at Eclectic Gift Shop. The small shop was founded in 2017 by Nicola Bartlett, who may win the award for the proudest Bristolian in our city. The clue as to the theme of her shop is in its name. Have a browse on the shelves, which are packed with a huge selection of ideal gifts mostly from Bristol, from cards and arts, to magnets and mugs. You might have even bought this very book from Nicola!

Bristol Rovers and Bristol City fans will spot the prints of the Memorial Stadium and Ashton Gate. There are also themes well away from the tourist trail such as the Purdown BT tower or the Troopers Hill chimney. And if you don't want a Bristol bauble decorating your Christmas tree, you could get that other classic present with a Bristol twist: the Suspension Bridge on a pair of socks.

TIP: Room 212 on Gloucester Road is another brilliant shop for Bristol-specific gifts.

Address 51c High Street, Hanham, BS15 3DQ, www.eclecticgiftshop.co.uk // Getting there Bus 17 to Hanham // Hours Tue–Sat 10am–4pm (open daily in December) // Ages 4+

35_EDWARD VII OAK TREE

Nature versus man

In a battle of nature versus man, there's only going to be one winner, as this oak tree on Brandon Hill proves. Planted in 1902 to commemorate the coronation of King Edward VII, whoever was in charge of Bristol's parks back then either got their sums wrong or did not know how large oak trees grow, or did not appreciate that fully grown oaks are girthy trees.

In the century and a bit since Alderman C. E. L. Gardner, Lord Mayor of Bristol, planted the sapling, its trunk has outgrown the circular metal railings that surround it. In fact, some of the base of the tree and the metal once encircling it with plenty of room to spare are now fused together, nature having no regard for man's arbitrary boundaries.

This tree is just one of some 500 trees on Brandon Hill made up of almost 100 different species, from giant sequoia to golden rain tree to copper beeches, to another oak that is more than 250 years old. It's one of the best collections of trees in Bristol with many of them having labels to inform you what they are if you don't know the difference between a hazel and a horse chestnut, or an ash and an acer. Find free tree trail leaflets courtesy of the Friends of Brandon Hill group in dispensers around the park.

The Edward VII oak is close to the city council's Brandon Hill depot where you can sometimes see council staff at work with chainsaws; perhaps getting their own back in the battle of nature versus man as the tree continues to imperceptibly outgrow its superfluous confines.

> TIP: Feeding squirrels is one of the most fun things to do on Brandon Hill.

Address Brandon Hill, BS1 5RR //
Getting there Short walk from Cabot Tower,
5-minute walk from top of Park Street //
Hours Accessible 24 hours // Ages 4+

THIS OAK TREE
WAS PLANTED ON THE 6TH DAY OF DECEMBER,
1902, BY ALDERMAN C.E.L. GARDNER,
LORD MAYOR OF BRISTOL, 1901-2,
IN COMMEMORATION OF THE CORONATION OF
H.M. KING EDWARD VII.

36_THE ENERGY TREE

Charge your phone via the Sun

There is a tree on one corner of Millennium Square unlike any other. This tree has a trunk and leaves but it is made of metal. The *Energy Tree* is both an artwork and a renewable power source, with a sign next to it saying that it was 'designed and built by Bristolians, standing as a symbol of the urgent need to create positive and fair solutions to the climate crisis'. The leaves are actually solar panels and you once could charge your phone for free using the (now broken) charging points.

So who were these Bristolians who designed and built the *Energy Tree*? The body of the tree was created by the sculptor John Packer, while the 36 solar 'leaves' were hand-built by men and women working with the Bristol Drugs Project to recover from problematic drug and alcohol use. The solar panels took eight months to finish, with participants gaining useful practical skills, and their handiwork is now on permanent show.

The tree works by sunlight hitting the panels with the energy of the light converted to electrical energy. The energy is stored in batteries under the tree and the batteries then release the energy to power your phone.

TIP: Splash around in the water features in Millennium Square on a hot day.

On Millennium Square, the *Energy Tree* is on one of four raised beds that used to be barren before being planted with a whole collection of plants and also vegetables that can be picked when in season. This bed also contains a 'hoverfly hotel' – perfect for insects like bees, wasps, butterflies and hoverflies to nest in while transferring pollen between plants in the city centre.

Address Millennium Square, BS1 5SZ // Getting there
In the corner of Millennium Square next to the planetarium //
Hours Accessible 24 hours // Ages 2+

37_EXPLORE THE UNIVERSE

In the UK's only 3D planetarium

There is a silver ball on one corner of Millennium Square. It may look like a giant glitter ball, but this is in fact your passport to explore the universe. The ball is a planetarium, part of We The Curious, and it can take you to far-flung galaxies without leaving the comfort of your seat.

'Our venue is less SHHH and more playful,' says the website of We The Curious, far removed from a typical science centre. It's a place where the boundaries are removed between science, art, people and ideas. Explore the venue to your heart's content. Talk to a robot, turn yourself invisible, animate your own short film, but don't miss the UK's only 3D planetarium.

Under-sixes can become fully qualified space explorers, taking off from Earth in a rocket ship and zooming through the Solar System. Children aged seven and above can wear the 3D-specs to join in the search for extra-terrestrial life, discover the movement of stars, fly to distant worlds or learn how astronomers search for planets, with all shows led by an expert guide.

Back down to Earth, birds were more than likely to blame for a fire in April 2022 that broke out among the solar panels in the We The Curious roof. Everyone inside the building was evacuated safely but there was significant fire and water damage which means that We The Curious is not due to reopen until sometime in 2023. Every cloud has a silver lining, though. The heating and cooling systems needed to be replaced, so this has helped the charity's mission to become carbon neutral by 2030.

Address We The Curious, 1 Millennium Square, Anchor Road, BS1 5DB, +44 (0)117 9151000, www.wethecurious.org // Getting there Short walk from College Green // Hours Wed–Sun 10am–5pm, school holidays daily 10am–5pm // Ages 0+

TIP: While We The Curious is closed, look out for their pop-up experiences across Bristol.

38_ FAIRY DOORS

Find your own Neverland

If you have read *Peter Pan*, you will know very well that you have to truly believe in fairies, and clap your hands if you want to save Tinker Bell. The sassy fairy lives on in the books of J. M. Barrie, and also in the numerous spin-off films, some of which Tinker Bell stars in herself as we meet a whole host of other fairies, each with different skills.

So where would these fairies reside if they lived in Bristol? There is one place that is ideal, and where dozens of fairies have already set up home. Still here after a successful community campaign to prevent houses being built on the land in the 1980s, Arnos Vale Cemetery has 45 acres of beautiful natural landscape to explore.

For those who really like to explore, however, there is some magic to be found – and it is children who are the best at finding it. Because, look down and you'll find some of the entrances to tiny homes. Fairy doors at the bases of trees come in a variety of shapes and colours, but they have one thing in common: you won't be able to fit in them unless you are very small and possibly also have a pair of miniature wings.

Seeing as you are in a cemetery, there are of course also plenty of interesting graves to find. The first features an almost life-size footballer kicking a ball. This is James Sanders, who played for Bristol City, Crystal Palace, Rochdale and Exeter City. The second is an elaborate tomb with a dome on top, which is the resting place of Rajah Ram Mohun Roy, a social reformer known as the father of modern India.

Address Arnos Vale Cemetery, Bath Road, Arnos Vale, BS4 3EW,
+44 (0)117 9719117, www.arnosvale.org.uk // Getting there
15-minute walk from Bristol Temple Meads; bus 1, X39, 57,
178 or 349 to Bath Road // Hours Daily 9am–5pm // Ages 3+

TIP: Nearby Arnos Manor Hotel is reputed to be haunted.

39_ FARMS IN THE CITY

Get acquainted with nature

One-quarter of city-dwelling children have never seen a cow, according to a study published a few years ago. The poll from 2018 also found that 27 per cent of these children had not come face-to-face with a sheep either. You may or may not have heard of the phrase 'lies, damned lies and statistics' – but there is an easy way of rectifying this particular bit of data, and that is by visiting one of Bristol's trio of splendid city farms.

Just a stone's throw from Asda on East Street is Windmill Hill City Farm, which has community gardens, a variety of farm animals, a play area, picnic areas, and a café and farm shop. You might be lucky and arrive to find that some piglets or lambs have just been born. Elsewhere, look out for the playful Pygmy goats Pip and Bella, and a brood of hens whose eggs can be purchased from the café.

St Werburgh's City Farm also has the feeling of being in a world of its own far away from the hustle and bustle of the rest of Bristol. It is on a much smaller scale than Windmill Hill, which means that you can get well acquainted with the animals who live on the smallholding, which includes a range of livestock including sheep, goats and pigs bred for meat, and ducks and chickens kept for their eggs.

Bristol's newest city farm is in Hartcliffe, which reopened in the summer of 2022 under a new partnership with Windmill Hill and the charity Heart of BS13. So far there are a small number of farm animals kept for educational and therapeutic purposes and food production.

> TIP: Mina Road Park in St Werburgh's has a stream running through it and a play area.

Address Hartcliffe City Farm, Lampton Avenue,
BS13 0QH, www.hartcliffecityfarm.org.uk;
St Werburgh's City Farm, Watercress Road,
St Werburgh's, BS2 9YJ, www.swcityfarm.co.uk;
Windmill Hill City Farm, Philip Street, Bedminster,
BS3 4EA, www.windmillhillcityfarm.org.uk //
Getting there Check websites for directions // **Hours**
Opening times vary (check websites) // **Ages** 1+

40_ FEATHERED FRIENDS

Fed and watered

From families on houseboats to floating restaurants (see ch. 16), Bristol's harbour is used for a whole host of activities. And then there are its feathered residents, from geese to the gulls who many consider a menace. Look up high and you might spot a kestrel, which is known to nest in the Avon Gorge and on buildings close to the Cumberland Basin. Or the smaller black and white house martins, who visit Bristol from Africa each summer, collecting mud from the River Avon, which they use to make their nests under the eaves of buildings.

Did you know that the monarch owns all of the unclaimed swans in open water in England? So those swans in the Floating Harbour technically belong to King Charles, but in reality he only exercises ownership on certain stretches and tributaries of the River Thames. Bristol's docks flow into the River Avon, so the swans who reside here and often perform spectacular landings on the water won't be taken as crown property.

The mute swans can usually be found around Welsh Back and Bristol Bridge, and also often make themselves known while you're feeding the ducks. Two great spots for this are by the Harbour Inlet close to where the ferry crosses back and forth from the SS *Great Britain* (see ch. 46) or on the other side of the water close to the City of Bristol Rowing Club, whose slipway is popular with families of mallards. Do avoid bread when you feed these ducks. Bread isn't good for them. Instead, feed them food including sweetcorn, lettuce, peas, oats, seeds and rice.

Address Harbour Inlet, Millennium Promenade, BS1 5SY; City of Bristol Rowing Club, Albion Dockside Estate, Hanover Place, BS1 6TR // Getting there Harbour Inlet is a 5-minute walk from Millennium Square; City of Bristol Rowing Club is a 5-minute walk from Underfall Yard // Hours Accessible 24 hours // Ages 1+

GRAIN BARGE

TIP: The Kyle Blue is a boat that offers holiday rental accommodation.

41_FILWOOD CRAZY GOLF

Will you get a hole in one?

Filwood Crazy Golf brings a new meaning to the word crazy. If you think you've already seen the craziest crazy golf course, then think again! This course is most definitely unique, with each hole inspired by different members of the community. The idea for it came from lockdown, when local families made their own courses at home, which have now been recreated in the middle of Filwood Community Centre.

The nine holes cost just £1 to play, with clubs, balls and a scorecard provided. Don't expect a putting surface worthy of the British Open. This colourful course was made out of recycled materials by Knowle West charity re:work and a team of volunteers, and is a little rough and ready around the edges – but that is half its charm.

A yellow model of the Clifton Suspension Bridge makes up most of one hole, with others themed around books, sewing and photography. An old tyre has been fashioned into a rainbow loop-the-loop, while another needs just as much putting power to get your ball up a near-vertical slope. One of the bespoke rules here is not to stand on the bridge or the pool table – where players need to turn their club into a cue.

TIP: Jungle Rumble in Cabot Circus has two 18-hole crazy golf courses.

Knowle West residents Kimberlee, Niamh and Henry Daly made their own Pokémon-themed golf hole at home during the pandemic because Filwood Community Centre is a PokéStop on *Pokémon Go*. The seventh hole is an ode to this with a smiling Pikachu given pride of place. See if you can hit your ball right through the middle of his open mouth for a hole in one!

Address Filwood Community Centre, Barnstable Road, Knowle West, BS4 1JP, +44 (0)117 9149216, www.filwoodcentre.org.uk/crazy-golf // Getting there Bus M1 to Filwood Broadway // Hours Mon–Thu 10am–3pm & Wed–Fri 3.30–6.30pm // Ages 4+

42_ FLYING SAUCERS

Paint a memory to last a lifetime

Walk into Flying Saucers, and the creative possibilities are almost endless. Just look at the bulging shelves, where more than 100 items are waiting for you. From plates, bowls and mugs, to unicorns, fairies and dinosaurs, there will be something here for you. The shapes are pre-made, but what you put on them is entirely up to you; just remember that the larger the item, the more expensive it is.

You do the painting and the professionals do the glazing and fir- ing, meaning that your unique ceramic creation can be brought home to become a family heirloom. Talking of heirlooms, baby footprints are a speciality here: all you need is a baby whose tiny feet can be transferred onto a picture frame, mug, teapot or just about anything else to remember when the tiny terror was even more tiny.

Mindfulness is a popular term these days, but it could easily have been invented to refer to the transcendental state that you can get into at Flying Saucers. Even the most energetic of children will find that a calmness descends with a piece of pottery and a paintbrush. Sit down with your chosen item and create your own masterpiece. You will find that the time will fly by as you get into the zone.

Every term-time Tuesday at Flying Saucers is Toddler Tuesday, with pre-schoolers and babies getting 10 per cent off and a free coffee for their adult. Birthday parties are also extremely popular here, with a special gift to the birthday child of a memento plate featuring the names (or thumb prints) of all of their friends.

Address 9 Byron Place, Clifton, BS8 1JT, +44 (0)117 9273666, www.flyingsaucers.co.uk/bristol // Getting there 3-minute walk from top of Park Street // Hours Tue–Sat 10am–5pm, Sun 11am–5pm // Ages 1+

43_ THE GEORGE MÜLLER MUSEUM

Find out what life was like as a Victorian orphan

Do you sometimes dislike your lessons at school? Teacher being strict or maths getting boring? Count your lucky stars that you are receiving an education at all. Two-hundred years ago, many children were sent to work from a young age. A pioneering orphanage in Bristol, giving poor children an education, was criticised for raising them above their station and for robbing factories, mills and mines of the cheap labour on which they relied.

The place where this orphanage was located is still almost entirely intact, but now contains private flats as well as the George Müller Museum, where you can find out more about his work and what life was like as an orphan. Remarkably, Müller cared for 10,000 orphaned children in Bristol during the Victorian era, first at a home on Wilson Street in St Paul's and then at a larger site in what was then outside the city at Ashley Down, with his name living on in several roads. A devout Christian, Müller was born in Germany and was a rebel during his own childhood, gambling and drinking before his life changed when he found religion.

At the museum you can try on the uniforms worn by the children who lived here. The older girls in the homes used to help make these clothes, which were often the only clothing the children had: three suits for boys and three dresses for girls. You can also see school books that were used in lessons, gavels that were hit on the desk by teachers to get pupils' attention, and wooden clubs that were swung by the boys in synchronised exercises.

Address 45–47 Loft House, College Road, Ashley Down, BS7 9FG, +44 (0)117 9245001, www.mullers.org/museum // Getting there 10-minute walk from Gloucester Road; bus 70 to Ashley Down Road // Hours Mon–Fri 10am–4pm // Ages 5+

44_THE GEORGIAN HOUSE MUSEUM

Explore life both above and below stairs

The Georgian House Museum treads a delicate balance between displaying the opulence of a wealthy merchant's home and questioning where that wealth was built. This being Bristol, the man who this house belonged to was one John Pinney, a slave plantation owner. So it was not just servants who tended to the elegant formal rooms above, but also slaves, including Pero Jones after whom Pero's Bridge (see ch. 75) is named.

Stepping into the Georgian House is like going back in time more than 230 years. All of the rooms spread over four floors have been decorated as they would have been when George III was on the throne. The movers and shakers of Georgian society would have assembled here, with the dinner table set for an extravagant dinner party whose guests might have included the poets William Wordsworth and Samuel Taylor Coleridge.

Rooms upstairs include a bedroom from where Pinney could have seen ships returning. But it's downstairs where most interesting finds

are, such as the kitchen and housekeeper's rooms. Also look out for a hidden staircase that enabled servants to get upstairs without being seen.

One of the most intriguing areas of the Georgian House is a cold-water plunge pool in the basement, thought to have been used by the master of the house who clearly was up to date with the latest fashions. One of the diseases supposedly cured by cold-water bathing was gout, caused by too much cheese and alcohol; in other words, living the high life. So we shouldn't feel sorry for Pinney.

TIP: Almost opposite, St George's is a music venue reputed to have some of the best acoustics in the UK.

Address 7 Great George Street, BS1 5RR, +44 (0)117 9211362, www.bristolmuseums.org.uk // Getting there Short walk from Park Street // Hours 1 Apr–31 Dec Sat–Tue 11am–4pm // Ages 4+

45__THE GIANT'S CAVE

A legendary home with a view

According to Bristol folklore, the land on which our city now stands was once home to two giants by the name of Goram and Vincent. These giants both fell in love with the same woman, Avona, who promised to marry the first to drain a huge lake that once stretched from Bradford-on-Avon to what is now Bristol.

Goram, who lived in Blaise (see ch. 8), chose a route through the Henbury Hills, but the digging was thirsty work and he took a rest, falling asleep. Vincent meanwhile opted for the Downs. He kept digging, emerged at Sea Mills and won the beautiful maiden Avona's hand in marriage, whose name was given to his gorge: the Avon Gorge. Broken-hearted, Goram hurled himself into the River Severn and drowned, with his head and shoulders still able to be seen poking out of the estuary mud as the rocks of Flat Holm and Steep Holm.

St Vincent's Rocks near the Clifton Suspension Bridge (see ch. 28) bears the name of the victor, with a cave in the vertical cliff face his legendary home. His footsteps can even still be seen near the cave's opening 250 feet above the Avon Gorge and 89 feet below the cliff top. If you want to believe another story, the cave is a natural feature, but the 200-foot-long tunnel connecting it with Clifton Observatory (also home to the Camera Obscura, see ch. 18) was dug by William West in 1835. The tunnel through solid rock took West two years to complete. Be sure to watch your head when walking down the narrow tunnel to the cave; it certainly would have been a squeeze for any giant.

TIP: Goram & Vincent is the restaurant at Hotel Du Vin in Clifton, perfect for a special occasion.

Address Clifton Observatory, Litfield Road, Clifton, BS8 3LT, +44 (0)117 9741242, www.cliftonobservatory.com // **Getting there** Short walk from Clifton Suspension Bridge; bus 8 or 9 // **Hours** Daily Apr–Oct 10am–5pm, Nov–Mar 10am–4pm // **Ages** 6+

46_GO ALOFT

Step into the shoes of a Victorian sailor

If you ran away to sea today, you might imagine working on a superyacht, sailing around tropical islands. It's not all fun and games of course, but it's a whole lot better than the life of a sailor on the SS *Great Britain*, the largest passenger ship in the world when it launched in 1843. Isambard Kingdom Brunel's famous boat was a steam ship, but it also had sails, and one of the main jobs of a sailor was looking after these as she sailed around the globe 32 times: more than a million miles at sea!

Consider yourself lucky that, when you climb the rigging, you are on board a ship that is not going anywhere, rather than in the middle of the Atlantic Ocean in a storm. Step into the shoes of a Victorian sailor to get a feel of what it was like to be part of the ship's crew by climbing to more than 80 feet high. If you are brave enough, you can then edge out onto the main yard, which takes you 30 feet out across the dockyard below, giving you a view over Bristol that usually only a seagull can enjoy.

TIP: Brunel's own boathouse is now the Harbour House restaurant.

Climb back down to the deck and take your time to explore the rest of the SS *Great Britain*, which is officially the smelliest museum in the world! Passengers, crew and livestock lived and worked in the same space for up to 60 days at a time during the voyages to Australia, making it a particularly pungent place. So get ready for sights, sounds and smells including freshly baked bread in the bakery and the not-so-nice odours of horse manure in the forward hold, and even vomit in a stewardess' cabin.

Address SS *Great Britain*, Great Western Dockyard, Gas Ferry Road, BS1 6TY, +44 (0)117 9260680, www.ssgreatbritain.org/things-to-do/go-aloft // Getting there 10-minute walk from Wapping Wharf; bus M2 to Cumberland Road // Hours Nov–Mar Tue–Sun 10am–4.30pm, Apr–Oct Tue–Sun 10am–6pm, also Mon from 25 Jul–29 Aug // Ages 10+ is minimum age for Go Aloft

47_GOAT GULLY

Hairy conservationists hard at work

There are plants in the Avon Gorge that are found nowhere else in the world. And there is a very hard-working, committed and never complaining team who allow them to flourish.

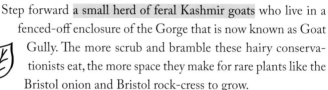

Step forward a small herd of feral Kashmir goats who live in a fenced-off enclosure of the Gorge that is now known as Goat Gully. The more scrub and bramble these hairy conservationists eat, the more space they make for rare plants like the Bristol onion and Bristol rock-cress to grow.

The goats do a fantastic job of eating the invasive scrub, but aren't particularly keen on interaction with two-legged visitors to their domain. If you see them, be sure not to approach them or feed them: they have plenty of natural food, and if you feed them, they may become sick. If you don't happen to see them on your visit to their home in the Gorge, look out for telltale signs of their presence. You guessed it: poo! Also in their home, look out for a castle turret. This is in fact a ventilation tower for the railway line in a tunnel below.

Within this area, goats are better at removing scrub than humans are, and they can also do the labour-intensive job all year round. These particular billy goats were chosen as they prefer to eat scrubby, woody vegetation, and they also suit the steep terrain. Without the goats' nibbling, trees and scrub would begin to grow, killing off the majority of the rare plants. These four-legged professionals play a crucial role in Bristol's commitment to tackling the ecological emergency and protecting the unique ecosystem of the Avon Gorge.

> TIP: Circular Road and Ladies Mile are popular places to run and cycle.

Address Clifton Downs, BS9 1FG, www.avongorge.org.uk // Getting there The gulley can be accessed via a path off Circular Road; 15-minute walk from Clifton Suspension Bridge // Hours Accessible 24 hours // Ages 5+

48_ GOLDEN HILL COMMUNITY GARDEN

Make your own fun in the open air

Golden Hill. Sounds tempting doesn't it? The hill may not be paved with gold, but there is still plenty sparkling here that enables you to enrich your soul, if not fill up your piggy bank with precious metal. 'We believe in child-led play, silliness, falling over and making our own fun,' says Lucy Mitchell from Golden Hill Community Garden, a place that she describes as an accessible allotment and edible forest. Anyone is welcome to get involved here, with the belief that everyone benefits from having the opportunity to grow their own food. There are numerous opportunities for children as well as adults with learning difficulties, with volunteers being the glue that holds everything together.

Golden Adventure Days give kids from 5 to 12 the chance to 'live the story', with themed days over the years based on pirates, Robin Hood, Harry Potter, dinosaurs and more. They promise a unique mix of outside fun, games, storytelling, costume making, activities and pizza cooked in a giant frog. Yes: pizza cooked in a giant frog!

After-school club for children in Years 1 to 6 ranges from den building to raft making, flower picking to fire starting. And for the youngest green-fingered participants, the Golden Buds parents and toddlers group also involves loads of outdoor activities, the chance to wander off and explore, as well as playing in the digging bed and helping water the plants.

Address On the allotments at the end of Monk Road, Bishopston, BS7 8NE, +44 (0)7506 905394, www.thegoldenhillcommunitygarden.com // Getting there Through the gates at the end of Monk Road, behind Bishop Road School and Horfield Prison // Hours Wed 10am–4pm; check website for weekly and school holiday activities // Ages 1+

TIP: There are a playground and tennis courts at the nearby Ardagh.

49_GOLF AT ASHTON COURT

Play golf three different ways

Make your way to the activity hub at Ashton Court and you will see people wielding a variety of implements all associated with the game of golf. You would expect a few golf clubs and a ball: there are two 18-hole pitch and putt courses here. But you will also likely see a few Frisbees and some colourful footballs, with these now also able to be thrown and kicked if you decide to play disc golf or foot golf.

If you want to play golf with traditional clubs and a golf ball, there is one flat course and another hillier course for players who would like more of a challenge. Both are par-three courses with no booking required. Simply turn up with your own clubs and balls or hire them for a refundable deposit. First stop, Ashton Court. Second stop, the Augusta Masters!

Like padel (see ch. 77), which combines tennis and squash to create a brand-new sport, the clue about foot golf is in the name. Players need to kick a size-five football into a hole in as few shots as possible, following golf's scoring system where the lowest individual or team score is the winner. So, rather than chipping a football over a wall of defenders towards a goal, you might chip your ball over a bunker towards the flag.

And then there's disc golf. Just have a look on YouTube for some incredible skills and try to replicate those yourself with a deft flick of the wrist as you send your disc spinning towards the metal target. A roll after it has landed can take the disc just as far as a throw, so give it your best shot!

Address Ashton Court Estate, BS8 3TX, +44 (0)117 9738508, www.bristol.gov.uk/residents/museums-parks-sports-and-culture/sports-and-fitness/golf // Getting there Bus X3 or X4; plenty of cycle racks next to the Golf Café // Hours Daily 8am–5.30pm // Ages 6+

TIP: Look for the head of the mythical giant Goram in Ashton Court.

50_GORILLA SHENANIGANS

Pranks, paintings and poo

There is a series of 'stairs to nowhere' at Bristol Museum & Art Gallery which used to connect the museum with the neighbouring Wills Memorial Building. It was through this former doorway in 1956 that students from the University of Bristol broke in and stole the taxidermied Alfred the Gorilla. After a few days, Alfred was left in a nearby doctor's waiting room. Alfred is still one of the most popular exhibits in the museum, having previously been a resident at Bristol Zoo for 18 years – where he was often walked around the former grounds in Clifton wearing a woolly jumper and was said to dislike bearded men and double-decker buses.

Find Alfred on the second floor of the museum, close to the horse-drawn Romany gypsy caravan, also known as a vardo, which is another of the most well-known displays. Parents traditionally slept on the bed inside the vardo, children in a cupboard underneath it, and older children under the wagon protected by tarpaulin round the wheels. Consider yourself lucky if you have your own bed in your own bedroom.

Elsewhere in the museum you can explore life in Ancient Egypt, finding children's toys from thousands of years ago and learning about everyone from pharaohs to farm labourers and fishermen in both life and the afterlife. Be sure also not to miss the collection of dinosaurs and sea dragons, including the Bristol dinosaur – a Thecodontosaurus – which was found during quarrying on the Downs. If you look closely you can even find some fossilised dinosaur poo.

Address Bristol Museum & Art Gallery, Queen's Road, BS8 1RL, +44 (0)117 9223571, www.bristolmuseums.org.uk/bristol-museum-and-art-gallery // **Getting there** Short walk from Park Street // **Hours** Tue – Sun 10am – 5pm // **Ages** 3+

Stairs to Nowhere
Stone with metal and wood railing

These stairs, seemingly disappearing into a wall, once led to a connecting door between the Museum & Art Gallery and the University of Bristol's Wills Building.

In 1956, students from the university used this door to break into the museum and steal 'Alfred the Gorilla'. Alfred was a very famous resident of Bristol Zoo Gardens until his death in 1948, from which time his taxidermied skin has been displayed in this building. After a few days of being 'in hiding', Alfred was left in a nearby doctor's waiting room and so was returned to the museum.

Today he is still a popular exhibit in the wildlife galleries upstairs. The names of the students behind Alfred's kidnapping only came to light in 2010.

TIP: Almost opposite the museum is Pizza Bianchi, where generous wedges of pizza can be bought by the slice.

51_GROMIT UNLEASHED

Bristol's world-famous Plasticine residents

Millions of pounds have been raised for the Grand Appeal – the Bristol Children's Hospital charity – thanks to sculpture trails featuring giant versions of Bristol's world-famous Plasticine residents. You can still see Wallace, Gromit and Shaun the Sheep in various locations, including 'Private Gromit' on Upper Maudlin Street opposite its junction with Colston Street.

Wallace & Gromit creators Aardman have their headquarters and studios in Bristol, and first allowed the use of their beloved characters to raise funds via the Grand Appeal to build a new children's hospital. The first Gromit Unleashed sculpture trail took place in 2013, with an auction of the 80 figures raising an extraordinary £2.3 million. Shaun in the City saw 120 sculptures of Shaun the Sheep appearing throughout Bristol and also London, while Gromit Unleashed 2 took place in 2018.

The fun-loving spirit of the trails lives on in the Gromit Unleashed shop in Cribbs Causeway, with all proceeds supporting Bristol Children's Hospital and the Neonatal Intensive Care Unit at St Michael's Hospital.

In the summer of 2023, it will be unicorns on display in Bristol as part of Unicorn Fest. Each statue will be decorated by a different local artist and this time money will be raised for Leukaemia UK. Until then, look out for unicorns already located across the city, including on opposite ends of City Hall, on the bow of the SS *Great Britain* (see ch. 46) and on Bristol's coat of arms, best seen above Old India restaurant on St Nicholas Street.

> TIP: Outside the Children's Hospital, a huge artwork called Lollipop Be-Bop has been compared to quidditch goalposts.

Address Gromit Unleashed shop,
The Mall, Cribbs Causeway,
BS34 5DG, +44 (0)117 9594201,
www.grandappeal.org.uk/gromit-
unleashed // Getting there Bus 1, 2,
3, 4, 73, 75 or 76 // Hours Mon–Fri
9.30am–8pm, Sat 9am–8pm,
Sun 11am–5pm // Ages 2+

52__HARBOUR RAILWAY

Travel back to the age of steam

Bristol is the only city in the UK with a public passenger steam railway right in its heart, that runs alongside a historic harbour. Steam train rides leave from M Shed (see ch. 62) most weekends, but be sure to check the timetables. Choose a trip to the SS *Great Britain* (see ch. 46) or alongside the New Cut to Vauxhall Bridge (which appears in the first scene of *Skins* for fans of the Channel 4 show).

Your trip will be powered by two Bristol-built steam engines, *Henbury* and *Portbury*, who both served on the docks railway system at Avonmouth. Like *Thomas*, they are tank engines, which means that they carry extra water for their boilers in a tank. To be precise, they are saddle tank engines because the water is in a tank over the top of the boiler, like a saddle on a horse. No need for a saddle to sit on during your ride. You will sit in an open-top wooden wagon.

The Harbour Railway has been serving Bristol since it was built by the Great Western Railway in the 1870s, and remained in use as a goods railway for over 100 years. A tunnel once connected the Harbour Railway with Temple Meads. The tunnel entrance and steps up to a footbridge that once crossed the line here can still be seen close to the Ostrich pub on Lower Guinea Street in Redcliffe.

If the trains are not running when you visit, borrow 20p to see models of a steam train and its wagons go round a circular track on the M Shed's ground floor. Close by, you might be able to see *Henbury* in her sidings, waiting patiently for her next journey.

Address M Shed, Princes Wharf, Wapping Road, BS1 4RN, +44 (0)117 3526600, www.bristolmuseums.org.uk/m-shed/whats-on/train-rides; buy tickets from the ticket office by the M Shed railway platform close to Prince Street // Getting there Short walk from M Shed or from Prince Street bridge // Hours These vary, so check the website; pre-booking is recommended // Ages 2+

TIP: The Severn Beach Line from Temple Meads is a superb little suburban railway.

53_HENGROVE PLAY PARK

Fun for children of all ages

When you arrive at Hengrove Play Park, the first thing that you are likely to see is a huge 40-foot-high dome. Inside there is a world of webs, tunnels, slides and suspended cages. It's a big moment for a little person when they first pluck up courage to enter what it is officially called the 'Jungle Dome' – but it's certainly not the only thing that children of all ages can get up to in one of Bristol's biggest play areas.

Hengrove Play Park is split into various distinct spaces, from a sand and water area for the smallest kids featuring a sandpit, water features and mini digger, to a basketball court and skatepark for older children. Elsewhere, a toddlers' area has a pirate ship, playhouse and car, while the 'Teen Zone' includes a 65-foot-long zip slide and spinning discs; and the 'Challenge Zone' has a climbing pyramid, climbing wall and a giant hamster wheel. On Thursday and Sunday mornings from 9.30am to 10.30am, disabled children are able to exclusively enjoy the play park with their siblings and family.

While you're here, head to Hengrove Park, where part of the runway of the original Bristol Airport can still be seen. It was in use from 1930 to 1957 and was particularly important in World War II when it was one of the few airports in England for civilian flights. Secret agents are likely to have flown here from Lisbon in neutral Portugal during the war. The last scheduled services took passengers to the Channel Islands, the Isle of Wight and the Isle of Man.

Address Hengrove Way, Hengrove, BS14 0HR, +44 (0)117 9222100 // Getting there Bus M1 to Hengrove Park // Hours Oct–Mar Wed & Fri–Sun 10am–5pm, Thu 10.30am–5pm; Apr–Sep Tue, Wed, Fri & Sat 10am–6pm, Thu & Sun 10.30am–6pm (skatepark open at all times) // Ages 1+

TIP: Popular CBeebies show *Andy's Adventures* is filmed at the Bottle Yard Studios in Hengrove.

54_HENRIETTA LACKS STATUE

She really is immortal

'To all the unrecognised Black women who have contributed to humanity, you will never be forgotten.' That's the inscription on the bronze statue of Henrietta Lacks by artist Helen Wilson-Roe, the first public statue of a Black woman made by a Black woman to be permanently installed in the UK.

Lacks changed the course of modern medicine, but she did not know it during her short life. In fact, her contribution to medical advances is still in use today, more than 70 years after the mother of five children from Virginia in the USA died of an unusually aggressive form of cervical cancer. From her humble beginnings, however, came immortality. During surgery, a sample of cells was taken from her tumour and sent to a laboratory. They were found to be the first living human cells ever to survive and multiply outside the human body.

They formed the first human cell line able to reproduce for ever, opening the door to all sorts of research and experiments on cell behaviour. This led to many breakthroughs in medicine, including the development of the polio vaccine, chemotherapy, gene-mapping, IVF and cloning.

But Henrietta's cells were taken without her or her family's knowledge or consent; it was only by accident that, in 1975, her family found out about her legacy. The 'HeLa' cells are still used in almost every major hospital and science based university in the world, including the University of Bristol – who commissioned her sculpture in 2021 and used the cells most recently for Covid-19 research.

TIP: Can you spot the metal monkey at the top of Cantocks Steps?

Address Royal Fort
Garden, Tyndall Avenue,
Kingsdown, BS8 1UH //
Getting there 5-minute
walk from top of Park
Street // Hours Accessible
24 hours // Ages 4+

55_ HOLLOW

Be surrounded by all the world's trees

It might look like a giant game of Jenga gone wrong, but *Hollow* is in fact a miniature forest. The wooden blocks for Jenga begin as alder trees, which grow primarily on the west side of the Cascade Mountains in the states of Washington and Oregon in the USA; and a sample of alder tree is contained somewhere within what has also been called a modernist grotto, big enough to fit two people inside at a squeeze, where you will be surrounded by 10,000 unique tree samples gathered from across the globe.

These samples include the oldest tree in the world, a tree that survived a nuclear blast and many trees that are now extinct. The intricate structure – with a hollow interior described by its architects as 'an introverted and meditative space' – represents our planet's history and evolution through time. Thousands of conjoined wooden blocks of differing sizes come from almost every tree on Earth, with openings on top of the sculpture letting in just enough natural light to create the dappled light effect of a forest canopy.

The artist behind *Hollow* is Katie Paterson, who has also broadcast the sounds of a melting glacier live, created a light bulb to simulate the experience of moonlight, and sent a recast meteorite back into space. An artwork of hers unveiled in 2022 at Apple's new headquarters in California shares similarities with *Hollow*. In an olive grove next to the visitor's centre at Apple Park are cylinders of pure cast glass made of sand collected from all the deserts on Earth.

Address Royal Fort Garden, Tyndall Avenue, Kingsdown, BS8 1UH, www.hollow.org.uk // **Getting there** 5-minute walk from top of Park Street // **Hours** Accessible 24 hours // **Ages** 4+

TIP: Find 2,500 different species of trees at Westonbirt Arboretum, 25 miles from Bristol.

56_JEEVAN SWEETS

100 per cent vegetarian and 100 per cent delicious

You might hear the whir of machines coming into the shop at Jeevan's from a room next door. Hidden from view, or sometimes just able to be glimpsed through an open door, is the kitchen where most of the delicious creations lining the shelves are all made by hand. It's a family affair here as well, with uncles and aunts working alongside nieces and nephews, all under the watchful gaze and magnificent beard of proprietor Jagtar Singh Kandola.

Jeevan's sells an all-vegetarian selection of mithai (Indian sweets), which are available throughout the year but are especially popular at festival time such as Diwali and Gurpurab, or for special occasions such as weddings. Packed full of mithai, one of the counters looks like a rainbow: try the red strawberry burfi, the orange gajrella, the yellow coconut chum chum or the green pistachio kalakand. And it just carries on, with many of the sweets here made from traditional recipes passed down through the generations.

Elders from Easton and Eastville pop in from their homes around the corner, and other customers travel to Jeevan's from across Bristol for the mithai or their legendary samosas with a crispy outer shell surrounding potato, peas and carrots. There are almost 100 languages spoken in Bristol, and you will hear many of them if you stay here long enough, perhaps eating a mithai or samosa before you've even got out of the door. The samosas especially taste best when they are as fresh as possible, from the kitchen to your mouth in seconds.

Address 415–417 Stapleton Road, Easton, BS5 6NE, +44 (0)117 9517688, www.jeevansweets.co.uk // Getting there 5-minute walk from Stapleton Road railway station; bus 24 or 48 // Hours Mon, Wed–Sat 10.30am–9pm, Sun 10.30am–8pm // Ages 4+

TIP: Royate Hill in Eastville is a nature reserve partly on top of a railway viaduct.

57_KIDS' COOKERY CLASSES

Delicious and nutritious home cooking

Volcanoes are often created in Knowle West. Fortunately, lava doesn't spill out onto Daventry Road. Instead, an egg is cracked into the volcano crater that has been made by a fork in a pile of flour. It's the first few minutes of a kids' cookery class, and making the pasta from scratch is the first task for today's class. After volcanoes, it is time to make a giant snake from bread dough the length of the large table that will eventually become bread rolls.

The young chefs are kneading, mashing, rolling and chopping. All learning new skills that could stand them in good stead for the rest of their lives. Everyone taking part in these classes eats what they make, with some of the ingredients coming from the garden outside. And if they don't like the pasta, they'll be sure to love the bread rolls, especially when they come fresh out of the oven and are slathered with a slice of butter.

TIP: Get one of the best views across Bristol from the top of the Northern Slopes.

The priority here is always for the children to eat, with recipe kits being prepared to send out to households across Bristol as the class is happening. One-day cookery workshops take place in the school holidays, with monthly classes on a Saturday for parents and their children to cook together.

'Right folks, we're all doing very well,' says Square Food Foundation founder Barny Haughton to the class. Barny started running cookery classes at his former restaurants before opening Square Food in Knowle West with the mission of reducing hunger, improving health, and bringing people together through food and cooking.

Address Square Food Foundation, The Park, Daventry Road, Knowle West, BS4 1DQ, +44 (0)117 4622686, www.squarefoodfoundation.co.uk // Getting there Bus 91 to Daventry Road // Hours Check website for workshop dates // Ages 7+

58_LASER FUSION

Let battle commence!

Put on your pack, head down to the 'airlock' and let battle commence! Allow your eyes to become accustomed to the gloom and then either work by yourself or within teams to shoot the opposition with your laser gun. Look out for the flashing lights from the packs on other players' shoulders: one of the places where you can hit them with your laser; and if they hit you, you know who it was even if they sneakily shoot you in the back as their name (or nickname) is displayed on your own gun. Damn that Darth Vader! Curse that Cookie!

No running is allowed during the game but hiding behind walls, turrets and towers most definitely is if you want to pick off the opposition one by one. You can use tactics or no tactics at all. And at the end of each game, you will get your own scorecard to take home showing exactly who you zapped and who zapped you.

If you become a Laser Fusion fanatic, Kids Club takes place every Sunday morning from 10am to noon, with as many games as you want to play in those two hours and the best thing: unlimited squash! Get your own membership card and a unique tag that unlocks your gun.

Also within Laser Fusion is the ClueHQ escape room, suitable for children aged 10 and over. Groups of two to six people are locked inside a room and given 60 minutes to work as a team, searching for clues and solving puzzles in order to escape in time. Escape room themes here include an underground bunker, the long-lost tomb of 'Cluetankhamun' and a mystery computer virus.

TIP: Look out for the large red doors: a clue from when this building was a fire station.

Address Silver Street, BS1 2AG, +44 (0)117 9293699, www.laserfusion.info // Getting there 3-minute walk from St Nick's Market // Hours Mon–Sat 10am–10pm, Sun 10am–9pm // Ages 6+

59_ LEANING TOWER OF TEMPLE

Bristol's own Leaning Tower of Pisa

When workers were employed to pull down dangerous buildings after the Bristol Blitz of World War II, they were ready to demolish Temple Church, which had been gutted by German incendiary bombs. Their reasons seemed sound: the church's tower was leaning at a dangerous angle, so it needed to be made safe and demolished. But then, fortunately, somebody told them that the tower had been leaning like this for almost as long as it had been standing.

The tower leans five feet out of the vertical and has an intriguing story behind it of people who dared to battle against gravity: Bristol's own version of King Canute, who attempted to control the tide. Work on the tower began in the 1390s, then halted when the tower started to lean. But a little wobble wouldn't stop them, so building work was optimistically resumed a few decades later. This time, the tall top stage was added with a deliberate correction of the leaning angle as the masons tried to build a true vertical stage on top of the leaning base. But now this top stage is also not vertical, as the base has kept on increasing its lean! So it has been left leaning precariously ever since.

The original church on this site had no tower, but another interesting story. It was built in the early 12th century by the Knights Templar, an order of warrior monks, who were heavily armed and dedicated to holy war. The Templars devoted themselves to defending Christian pilgrims on their way to Jerusalem, and also probably invented banking – but that's another story!

> TIP: Bristol has some strange and funny street names, like Granny's Lane and Happy Lane. Right near the church is Petticoat Lane.

Address Temple Church, Victoria Street, BS1 6HS, www.english-heritage.org.uk/visit/places/temple-church // Getting there 5-minute walk from Bristol Temple Meads // Hours Entry into the church is free during daylight hours // Ages 5+

60_LEIGH WOODS

A wildlife haven just outside the city

If you ask 20 different people their favourite things to do in Leigh Woods, you'll probably get 20 different answers. Perhaps it will be the natural play trail that looks as though it has grown organically from the landscape. Clamber through hollowed-out logs, balance across a bridge or swing in a web-style basket that hangs from two of the wood's old beech trees.

Perhaps it will be finding the best place for a picnic, maybe sitting on the carved wooden sofa. Perhaps it will be a game of hide-and-seek. Or it might be looking for animal tracks. Then maybe it will be exploring the two massive banks and ditches that were built as part of an Iron Age camp.

Stretch your legs to find some of the oldest and most beautiful trees in Bristol. Ancient trees are living archaeology, providing evidence of historic land use, such as a wood pasture or royal hunting forest, as well as having amazing character and beauty, and being incredibly rich in wildlife. Or get on your bike to cycle down mountain bike trails suitable for beginners, that join up with the trails at nearby Ashton Court (see ch. 32).

Look out for animals such as roe deer and foxes. Many species of mice and voles live here, and if you're very lucky you might even spot a grass snake. The woods are also a very rich site for insects, including moths, butterflies and beetles. And at dusk, look out for bats, which make their winter roosts in the wood's trees and caves. What will become your favourite thing to do in Leigh Woods?

Address Leigh Woods, BS8 3QB, +44 (0)117 9731645, www.nationaltrust.org.uk/leigh-woods // Getting there 5-minute walk from Clifton Suspension Bridge; bus X3 or X4 towards Portishead; very limited car parking // Hours Open dawn to dusk // Ages 2+

61_ LOOK UP, LOOK DOWN

An architectural treasures trail

It's often said that you can spot a tourist because they are the ones looking up at buildings. But everyone taking part in this architectural treasure trail needs to look down as well as up. The aptly named Look Up, Look Down is like a giant jigsaw puzzle. Find the missing pieces of a pattern and the architectural features that inspired them.

Begin on Clare Street where it meets St Stephen's Street to find on the ground a pattern grid with shapes missing from the dozen colourful squares. There are mythical creatures including a sphinx, unicorn and dragon; animals it's unusual to find in Bristol such as a lion and an elephant; and symbols like a heart, a leaf and a scallop shell. Each of the shapes missing from the pattern grid can be found among the historic thoroughfares of the Old City.

So, without giving the whole game away, the unicorn is on St Stephen's Street close to a building on which is Bristol's coat of arms, featuring a pair of the legendary beasts on either side of Bristol Castle (see ch. 13) and the Matthew (see ch. 64). Further down this same road is a drinking fountain featuring Queen Victoria, which was installed to celebrate her 40th birthday. Water was dispensed from a scallop shell under Victoria's head.

Made from long-lasting thermoplastic, the trail by artists Sophie and Rob Wheeler was commissioned by Bristol City Council to celebrate the pedestrianisation of the Old City, and to create playful opportunities for people to explore the area and its history.

Address Find the pattern grid outside Pho, Clare Street, BS1 1YA, www.visitbristol.co.uk/oldcityarts, or download it from www.visitbristol.co.uk by searching for Look Up, Look Down // Getting there Short walk from fountains or from St Nick's Market // Hours Accessible 24 hours // Ages 3+

TIP: Stanfords book shop on Corn Street has a well-stocked children's section.

62_ M SHED

A celebration of Bristolians

If Bristol Museum & Art Gallery (see ch. 50) is Bristol's mantelpiece, M Shed is its attic, full of items that have been accumulated over the years and thrown together seemingly at random. But it is all the better for its ramshackle nature, expertly curated of course, and telling much of the story of our city through the people who have lived and continue to live here.

So, in one corner of a room there is a bust of Conrad Finzel, like so many before and since him an adopted Bristolian. His bust used to be on display in the Shakespeare pub in Totterdown, where it was known as Mr Ed, and often used to wear sunglasses. He is a man from Bristol's past in the same museum as displays celebrating current sons and daughters, including poet and performer Vanessa Kisuule, writer Nikesh Shukla, Winter Olympics bronze medallist Jenny Jones, and world champion snooker player Judd Trump. There's also some bloke called Banksy, whose *Grim Reaper* stencil originally daubed on the side of the Thekla in a stealth mission by boat is on display.

Among the photos and memorabilia, you can learn about parts of Bristol that even people who have lived here their whole lives may not have visited. Discover the origin story of Avonmouth, coal mining in Easton, Knowle West's former cinema and what was once Europe's largest cigarette factory in Hartcliffe. On the floor next to the green double decker bus on the ground floor that you can climb on board, there is a huge aerial photograph of the city so you can find some of these places yourself.

Address Princes Wharf, Wapping Road, BS1 4RN, +44 (0)117 3526600, www.bristolmuseums.org.uk/m-shed // Getting there 10-minute walk from fountains // Hours Tue–Sun 10am–5pm // Ages 4+

TIP: If you're hungry after a visit to M Shed, head to nearby Wapping Wharf.

63_ MAKE FRIENDS WITH AN ALPACA

¿Cómo se llama?

What's the difference between an alpaca and a llama? Don't ask me, ask the team at Wolfridge Alpaca: if anyone knows, it's going to be them! Alpacas are the animal of choice here, and if you want, you can get up close and personal with these gentle creatures at this no-frills rustic attraction.

During the experience, you will pair up with a keeper to feed an alpaca or two – perhaps even from the palm of your hand. Feel their amazing fleeces, learn how to hold them and smile for the camera! Don't be put off by their bodily functions: these are animals of course. In the wild they are primarily found in Peru and Bolivia in South America, where humans have used them for transportation and fleece production for thousands of years.

It's free to enter the farm, and many locals visit just to sit in the café, which has a view of the animals. Only opening for the first time in February 2022, the café is in a large former hay barn, with regular craft workshops taking place here. These include making alpaca pom-poms and alpaca biscuit decorating. You can also just have a wander around the paddocks on a circular walking route without the need to pay for a special experience, with an information trail, map and quiz sheet costing just £1.

(Okay, so you've got this far in the chapter and you still want to know the difference between an alpaca and a llama? Both species are part of the camel family. Alpacas are smaller than llamas, with softer hair, making for better wool and they also tend to be more timid.)

Address Wolfridge Alpaca, Forty Acre Lane, Alveston, BS35 3QU, +44 (0)7443 894859, www.wolfridgealpaca.co.uk // Getting there Bus T1 to Alveston Church; cycle racks on site // Hours Tue–Sat 9.30am–5pm, Sun 10am–4pm; check website for details of workshops // Ages 2+

TIP: Old Down
Country Park
has play areas and
an animal park.

64_THE MATTHEW

All hands on deck

Climb aboard the *Matthew* and be transported back to 1497 when John Cabot sailed across the Atlantic on a boat that may or may not have looked like this, to make land in North America. Since it was built to mark 500 years of that famous voyage, the replica of the *Matthew* has become one of the most famous sights in the Floating Harbour. It makes regular trips throughout the year, sailing around the docks or up the Avon Gorge. But if you haven't got your sea legs on, you can take a look around while it is moored near Wapping Wharf, climbing the steps to the upper decks.

Built using as many traditional techniques as possible, the *Matthew* is a reconstruction of a caravel, popular in medieval times due to its speed and manoeuvrability. In Cabot's day, shipwrights did not produce plans to build their ships. So the reconstruction was based on archaeological evidence of ships and shipbuilding from the time, alongside contemporary illustrations and descriptions.

The original *Matthew* would most probably have been made of oak, larch and pine; the modern *Matthew* is built from oak and Douglas fir. Don't tell Cabot, but the replica of his ship also complies with 21st-century health and safety regulations. There are orange life rings on deck and even a diesel engine to give a bit more oomph when the wind in the sails is lacking. Following an ancient tradition, when the mast carrying those sails was originally raised, a genuine medieval gold coin was placed beneath it, where it remains to this day.

Address Princes Wharf, BS1 4RN, +44 (0)117 9276868, www.matthew.co.uk // Getting there Short walk from Wapping Wharf // Hours Apr–Oct Tue–Sun 10am–4pm, Nov–Mar Sat & Sun 10am–4pm // Ages 4+

TIP: Sit outside New Cut café for a great view of the hustle and bustle of the harbour.

65_MIRROR MAZE

You'll be amazed

It's difficult to get lost in the mirror maze at Royal Fort Garden. But it's easy to become discombobulated. Dozens of vertical polished steel plates (76 in fact) make up the maze, and once you enter, you experience the disorientating effect of multiple reflections. If you've ever wanted to play tag where there are six different versions of you, this is the place to do it! And only absolute hide-and-seek experts will be able to win a game here when almost every angle is visible.

The maze is actually a sculpture called *Follow Me* by Danish artist Jeppe Hein, a few hundred yards away from another artwork in Royal Fort Garden, *Hollow* (see ch. 55), that you can also step inside, but which has less room for running around in. *Follow Me* is at the bottom of a slope that is just the right angle for rolling down. When you roll your way to the sculpture, see if you can shout its name and avoid your follower as you dart around the maze. If you're small enough, you don't even have to follow the paths.

TIP: Listen to your heart on a 10-foot-tall wooden sign at Royal Fort Garden.

It's certainly a stretch to call the 20-foot by 20-foot square a labyrinth, but Hein himself has described it as one, so who are we to argue? Commissioned as part of the University of Bristol's centenary celebrations in 2009, he was inspired by the early 19th-century history of the gardens, which created the illusion of an uninterrupted landscape rolling down to the river; with pathways hidden below retaining walls, and trees and shrubs softening the view of the city and screening the 'unsightly rows of houses'.

Address Royal Fort Garden, Tyndall Avenue, Kingsdown, BS8 1UH, www.bristol.ac.uk/external-estate // Getting there 5-minute walk from top of Park Street; bus 9 to Tyndall Avenue // Hours Accessible 24 hours // Ages 2+

66_MOUNTAIN BIKING

The most fun you'll have on two wheels

On a rainy day in Bristol, on tarmacked city centre streets, you might spot a few mountain bikers completely covered in mud. How did they get like this? Probably on some epic mountain bike trails. (Just as an aside, did you know that tarmac was invented in Bristol? Engineer and road-builder John McAdam developed Tarmacadam – later known as tarmac – when a surveyor in the city. He also built Bridge Valley Road, which you might cycle up on your way to Ashton Court.)

Winding and weaving through the trees of Ashton Court, Leigh Woods and 50 Acre Wood, are a number of mountain bike trails suitable for beginners to experts. If you haven't taken a corner via a banked curve, this is the place to learn. Allow centrifugal force to be your friend, trust your suspension and have fun! In Ashton Court, you can find the easier Nova trail and the more difficult Super Nova trail; while in Leigh Woods, the Yer Tiz trail is a great place to start. Just make sure you always wear the right safety clothing, and only ride on the designated trails in the correct direction.

TIP: For a different mode of transport, Bristol Balloon Fiesta takes place at Ashton Court in August.

Don't have your own mountain bike? No problem. Pedal Progression, tucked away behind the golf café at Ashton Court, have hire bikes of all shapes and sizes. They even hire kids' seats that can fit onto the front of any adult mountain bike, and are suitable for children aged from two to five, giving the youngest riders their first taste of the trails. 5- to 14-year-olds can have coaching from Pedal Progression's expert staff, who also run regular girls-only sessions.

Address Ashton Court Estate,
BS8 3PX, +44 (0)117 9731298,
www.pedalprogression.com // **Getting
there** By bike of course; bus X3 or X4 //
Hours Opening times vary, so check
the website // **Ages** 5+

67_MRS POTTS

A chocoholic's paradise

Sit in the middle of Mrs Potts under a tree whose branches almost reach the ceiling and be careful not to eat the back of your seat while enjoying the hot chocolate and cakes on the table in front of you. Because the buttons holding the seat together look a lot like the chocolate buttons served with every drink and cake here in this chocolate lover's paradise. They're 38 per cent milk chocolate buttons to be precise, dark or white chocolate depending on what you order.

Watch the desserts being baked through a small window at the far end of the café, which in 2020 moved into larger premises on Park Street just a few hundred yards from their original home nearby. Michael and Jennifer Potts ran restaurants in Australia before opening Mrs Potts in Bristol with their daughter Amelia Pocock. The trio now also have cafés in Bath and Cardiff, with queues of sweet-toothed customers often forming outside their cafe – or 'chocolate bar' – in Bristol.

Half a dozen choices of hot chocolate are joined on the menu by deluxe milkshakes served with cookies and cream, toasted marshmallows or brownies. You might not be able to eat the buttons on your chair under the shade of the tree, but find them served on the cookies or cookie sandwiches, and generous slices of cake. Or get a sharing plate featuring a bit of everything. A hot day outside? Choose a decadent brownie ice cream sundae. For littler eaters, there are mini chocolate mousse pots with sprinkles on top, and white chocolate coated cake pops.

Address 50 Park Street, BS1 5JN, +44 (0)117 3021467, www.mrspottschocolatehouse.co.uk // Getting there 4-minute walk from College Green // Hours Daily 10am–8pm // Ages 6+

TIP: Find some second-hand bargains at the Vintage Thrift Store on Park Street.

68_MUD, MUD, GLORIOUS MUD

Keep things shipshape and Bristol fashion

Mud. If you're like Peppa Pig and enjoy jumping in muddy puddles, then you've come to the right place. But mud is not so much fun if it's your job to keep Bristol docks operational. And there's lots of mud: more mud enters the docks at Avonmouth on just one tide than the entire weight of cargo imported in a year.

Bristol docks are also known as the Floating Harbour because the water here on the original route of the River Avon is kept at a constant level, with the tidal section of the river carried by a channel still known as the New Cut, despite being dug more than 200 years ago. Pleasure boats have now replaced cargo ships, so the docks are as busy as ever, with Underfall Yard providing a picture-postcard view.

If not removed, mud – also known as silt – settles in the docks reducing their depth and making it difficult for ships to navigate. At the Underfall Yard Visitor Centre, budding engineers can play on magnet-operated games to help clear silt from the harbour, move a boat through a lock or prevent the docks from flooding. Close by, the human accumulator explains hydraulic power as visitors are lifted several metres upwards using the power of pumps. Science has never been so uplifting!

And pride of place in the middle of the visitor centre in the old hydraulic power house is a huge aerial photo of Bristol stretching from Netham Weir to Hotwells. Buttons allow places of interest such as the River Frome, Bathurst Basin and the Feeder Canal to be lit up, hopefully all clear of the menace of mud.

TIP: Don't be afraid of the full-sized knitted crocodile in the Underfall Yard Visitor Centre.

Address Underfall Yard Visitor Centre, Cumberland Road, BS1 6XG, +44 (0)117 9293250, www.underfallyard.co.uk // **Getting there** Nearest ferry stops are Nova Scotia Place or Cottage Inn; 1.5-mile walk from the city centre // **Hours** Easter–Oct Tue–Sun 10am–5pm, Oct–Easter 10am–4pm // **Ages** 4+

69_NINJA WARRIOR

From mini ninjas to masters

Type 'Ninja Warrior' into YouTube and you will find videos that have been viewed millions of times of superhuman women, men and children seemingly defying the laws of both gravity and physics as they race around a giant obstacle course. Even former NASA engineer and YouTuber Mark Rober has created a Ninja Warrior course in his back garden – although admittedly, that one was for squirrels.

But you no longer just have to watch Ninja Warrior online or on ITV from the comfort of your home. The giant obstacle course – with a few extra surprises thrown in for good measure – has leapt from the small screen to real life. The latest Ninja Warrior UK adventure park opened in Bristol in December 2022. Participants are invited to climb, balance, jump and swing across different obstacles, as well as a giant inflatable obstacle course. There is the 'warped wall' with dif-

ferent heights that you can work towards mastering, the inflatable 'Mount Sasuke' to clamber up and soft play areas for mini ninjas.

Within the 43,000 sq ft indoor facility, there are obstacles to suit all abilities. Some may look impossible to complete at first but have faith in yourself! Try, try and try again; and when you master that next obstacle, soak up that sense of achievement. You can also race friends and family, and Ninja Warrior is fast becoming a popular party venue. Be prepared to sweat and remember you can refuel in the café upstairs which also has the best view of the adventure park. Can you beat the wall?

Address Lysander Road, Patchway, BS34 5TX, www.ninjawarrioruk.co.uk/bristol // Getting there 5-minute walk from The Mall at Cribbs Causeway // Hours Mon–Thu 9am–8pm, Fri–Sun 9am–9pm // Ages 4+ (0+ for mini ninjas soft play)

TIP: Smyths Toys Superstore is almost next door.

70_NOAH'S ARK ZOO FARM

The UK's only creationist zoo

There are more than **100 species of animals** at Noah's Ark Zoo Farm – from alpacas to zebras, from fluffy rabbits to giant African elephants. There are also plenty of farm animals here on a site that was once a working dairy farm including sheep, pigs and Shetland ponies, who move between fields and barns throughout the different seasons.

Climb up looking towers to get some of the best views of the animals brought here from across the world, such as the African lion and the American bison. Get lost in the giant maze or hang upside-down like a monkey in the indoor and outdoor play areas. Watch a flying display by some **majestic birds of prey,** join in at feeding times, splash about in Welly Splash or go digging and scooping as you control your own digger by the Big Cat Sanctuary. For under-fives, Jungle Tots is a regular parent and toddler group providing a morning of soft play, crafts, animal handling and storytime.

Push open the door of the Noah's Ark Exhibition room, however, and you will find **something unexpected.** Noah's Ark Zoo Farm has the unusual distinction of being the UK's only creationist zoo. This means that its founders believe that humans did not descend from apes, but instead were created by God as it says in the Bible.

A 14-foot scale model of the ark in this room also gives a clue as to the name of the attraction, with information boards allowing you to make up your own mind about the truth or not of Noah, the ark and his saving of all the Earth's animals from **a flooded world.**

Address Clevedon Road, Wraxall, BS48 1PG, +44 (0)1275 852606, www.noahsarkzoofarm.co.uk // Getting there Bus X6 stops at the Noah's Ark Zoo Farm gate // Hours Feb–Nov daily 10.30am–5pm, Dec & Jan daily 10.30am–4pm // Ages 1+

TIP: Bristol's last working farm is Yew Tree Farm in Bedminster Down.

71_ OAKHAM TREASURES

A treasure-trove of retail memorabilia

Do you collect anything? Maybe playing cards, books or toys? Oakham Treasures is the culmination of one man's passion for collecting memorabilia throughout his life. Farmer Keith Sherrell began collecting farming paraphernalia in the 1960s as a sideline to his business of buying and selling used farm machinery. He started buying a bit more and selling a bit less, and the astonishing collection grew from there.

But you don't have to be a farming fanatic to enjoy it here. In the days before supermarkets, specialist shops lined every high street, and through Keith's interest in retail, you can now visit shops that your great-grandparents would have been familiar with, including an old grocery, haberdashery, hardware store, chemist, tobacconist, off licence and sweet shop (for a visit to an old-fashioned sweet shop still in operation, visit Treasure Island Sweets in St Nick's Market (see ch. 85)).

In this sweet shop, you will find a multitude of Fry's memorabilia, with merchandise and advertising campaigns, as well as many chocolate bars in their original packaging, that would have once been made in the Fry's factory in the centre of Bristol that later moved to Keynsham and became Cadbury's.

See if you can also find a number of well-known brands that are still going strong today, and many others now lost in the mists of time. Although not lost here at Oakham's Treasures thanks to Keith's magpie-like tendencies for collecting what were once throwaway purchases that are now rare glimpses into a lost era.

Address Portbury Lane, Portbury, BS20 7SP, +44 (0)1275 375236, www.oakhamtreasures.co.uk // Getting there Bus 88 // Hours Tue–Sat 10am–5pm // Ages 4+

WESTERN DAILY PRESS

FIRST ESTABLISHED · LARGEST CIRCULATION

BRISTOL

THE CHIEF NEWSPAPER AND BEST ADVERTISING MEDIUM IN THE WEST

TIP: Oakham Treasures has an on-site caravan park.

OAKHILL POST OFFICE

P
MON
PAR
IN
EXP

MESSENGERS

LICENSED TO SELL POSTAGE AND INLAND REVENUE STAMPS

YOU MAY TELEPHONE

POST OFFICE

POST OFFICE LETTER BOX.

NOTICE. LETTERS WHICH CONTAIN COIN IF POSTED AS ORDINARY LETTERS WILL BE CHARGED ON DELIVERY WITH A SPECIAL REGISTRATION FEE OF FIVEPENCE

V R

V R
POST OFFICE LETTER BOX

POST OFFICE

WOOLHO POST OFF

72_OTOMÍ

A magnificent melange of Mexican memorabilia

You might find a toilet for sale in Otomí. Not just any toilet either, but a fantastically colourful toilet base and cistern handmade in the Guanajuato region of Mexico by skilled artisans. Who needs a boring bathroom when a simple trip to the loo can transport you halfway around the world?

A visit to this shop that began life as a market stall is anything but boring. Otomí is named after the tribe that gave Otomí co-owners Louise Dark and Alex Orozco Luquin their first products: traditional paintings from Guadalajara, Alex's home city. From those first artworks, the business has grown quickly, but remained true to its original ethos of selling authentic Mexican products, from toilets to tortillas, wrestling masks to mirrors.

On a hot day – or even on a not-so-hot day – visit Otomí for their selection of paletas: all-natural, homemade, whole-fruit ice lollies. Or choose from a selection of food and drink, from Pulparindots (coated tamarind sweets filled with hot and salted tamarind pulp) to chilli hot chocolate. The products change regularly but you're always guaranteed to find plenty of Frida Kahlo iconography and enough Day of the Dead figurines to make your own skeleton army in time for 2 November.

'Our hope is that we have recreated a little piece of Mexico in the UK,' say Louise and Alex. 'We want your experience with us to be unique and hopefully nostalgic. Please do feel free to come into the shop in Bristol for an astonishing array of colour, aromas and a chat, even in Spanish!'

Address 4 Boyce's Avenue, Clifton Village, BS8 4AA, +44 (0)117 9732906, www.otomi.co.uk // Getting there Short walk from Victoria Square; bus 8 to Clifton Village // Hours Mon–Fri 10am–5.30pm, Sat 10am–6pm, Sun 11am–4pm // Ages 5+

HECHO EN

TIP: Reg the Veg on Boyce's Avenue is one of the best – and most photographed – green-grocers in Bristol.

73_ PAINTWORKS GRAND PRIX

Watch out for banana skins!

The competitors take to the start line. Anyone who has ever played *Mario Kart* will be familiar with the vehicles of Mario, Luigi, Yoshi, Princess Peach and Toad.

But what's this? There are some interlopers among the participants as the green light goes on and the race begins! First up are four PacMan characters looking decidedly suspicious. Behind them is the famous *Ghostbusters* van, and almost bringing up the rear is Sonic, with Donkey Kong in last place.

This is the Paintworks Grand Prix – with the pixelated characters harking back to the days of the Super Nintendo Entertainment System or the SNES for short (ask your parents). Look closely and those pixels are actually tiles; the painstaking work of mosaic artist Angus, whose handiwork can be found across Bristol where he incorporates more computer game characters including Street Fighter pugilists, as well as a Smurf, Space Invaders and R2D2. Originally a graffiti artist working on walls with more traditional spray paints, Angus then switched to tiles and mosaics and has found his forte, becoming a regular guest at the annual Upfest street art festival – where in 2022 he created a stunningly detailed Day of the Dead skull in Greville Smyth Park.

But back to the Paintworks Grand Prix... and they're off! Shy Guy immediately fires off a red shell towards King Boo. Luigi looks likely to move up the field until he is hit by a banana skin from Wario. And Yoshi takes the chequered flag, holding the gleaming gold trophy aloft on top of the podium!

Address Central Road, Paintworks, BS4 3AQ // Getting there Find Angus' work on the wall opposite the steps up to the Martin Parr Foundation // Hours Accessible 24 hours // Ages 3+

TIP: Princess Daisy emerges from a green pipe close to the main entrance to the Paintworks on Bath Road.

74_PALM TEMPLE

Almost all the colours of the rainbow

If you've ever wondered what it feels like to be inside a kaleidoscope, then this is your chance. Try to visit *Palm Temple* on a sunny day when the colours pop! There are reds, yellows, greens, blues and purples: almost all of the colours of the rainbow that, when the sun is shining, extend from the artwork like a multicoloured shadow. The calmness of the cedarwood structure, with a mirrored floor and panels like a stained-glass window, is sometimes only broken by the rustle of the trees in the courtyard outside.

TIP: For more rainbows, walk up the nearby Cantocks Steps.

Palm Temple is an artwork best experienced when you walk inside. It was made by Bristol-based artist Luke Jerram who you might know from *Play Me, I'm Yours*, pianos placed on streets across the world. Donated to the University of Bristol by Jerram, it was originally commissioned by Sky Arts as a celebration of the 600th anniversary of the dome of Florence Cathedral; with this dome cut in half and the two halves placed in parallel like two palms coming together.

Look up to find the 'extinction bell', suspended in the apex of the dome. The bell tolls 150 to 200 times a day at random intervals, indicating the number of species lost worldwide every 24 hours. Close to the artwork, next to the entrance to the chemistry building nearby, find a blue plaque honouring the scientists who discovered the precise nature of soil and rock samples from the Moon taken during Apollo missions. One of these scientists was Colin Pillinger, best known for later trying to land the Beagle 2 spacecraft on Mars.

Address University of Bristol chemistry precinct, Cantock's Close, BS8 1TS (What3Words location: spirit.often.jukebox) // Getting there 5-minute walk from top of Christmas Steps; bus 1, 2, 8, 9 or 79 to top of Park Street // Hours Accessible 24 hours // Ages 3+

75_PERO'S BRIDGE LOVELOCKS

Love them or loathe them?

Let's leave Bristol for a moment and travel across the English Channel to Paris where, in 2014, part of a bridge had to be closed when one of its metal grilles collapsed under the weight of thousands of locks. These 'lovelocks' are part of a relatively modern tradition whereby sweethearts inscribe their names or initials on a padlock, attach it to a public structure and throw away the key.

The Pont des Arts bridge in Paris now regularly has new lovelocks taken down, but at its equivalent in Bristol, the number continues to grow. Soon after he was elected as Bristol mayor in 2016, Marvin Rees said it was unlikely that the lovelocks on Pero's Bridge would be removed, calling them 'a part of the creativity and iconic sights' of the Floating Harbour. His comments came as a crowdfunder campaign to buy bolt cutters to get rid of the locks was gaining momentum, raising more than twice as much money as a rival campaign pledging to keep the locks. Do you love the locks or would you get rid of them if you could?

Pero's Bridge is currently the closest that Bristol has to a memorial to the enslaved men, women and children who made the city's merchants wealthy in the 17th and 18th centuries. Pero Jones and his two sisters, Nancy and Sheeba, were the property of a Bristol businessman who lived in what is now the Georgian House (see ch. 44). He lived and died a slave. This makes the locks on it even more problematic for some, being inappropriate to the memory of Pero Jones as well as being an eyesore.

Address Pero's Bridge, between Narrow Quay and Bordeaux Quay, BS1 5UH // Getting there Short walk from Millennium Square or from the fountains // Hours Accessible 24 hours // Ages 4+

TIP: Society Café
next to the bridge
was originally
a rope factory.

76_ PLANET ICE

Ice ice baby

University accommodation stands where, for 46 years, an ice rink was located above what is now the O2 Academy music venue. The ice rink opened in 1966 (the year when England men's football team won the World Cup at Wembley) but closed in 2012, the same year as the UK hosted the Olympics. For a few years, a temporary ice rink used to be built on Millennium Square every Christmas, but We The Curious stopped this as part of their mission to become a carbon-neutral venue (making something so cold requires a lot of heat).

So for almost a decade, Bristol did not have an ice rink to call its own – a sad indictment of the lack of any world-class sporting facilities we have compared with other cities. But all is not lost! Because in 2021, Planet Ice opened in Cribbs Causeway. This meant that Bristol's ice hockey team, the Pitbulls, were able to return after years of having to play home games in Oxford. An evening watching a game here is a fun way to spend a Saturday night. Just remember to wrap up warm.

If you want to get on to the ice yourself, there are plenty of opportunities at Planet Ice, with public skate sessions taking place seven days a week and evening disco sessions at the weekend. Want to have the coolest birthday party in town? Birthday parties here are *Beano*-themed. And if you want to improve your sliding skills, ice skating, ice hockey or ice dance lessons are all available here. There are also lessons available for young skaters aged three to five using penguins – yes, penguins!

Address Merlin Road, Cribbs Causeway, BS10 7SR, +44 (0)117 2130134, www.planet-ice.co.uk/locations/bristol // Getting there 5-minute walk from The Mall at Cribbs Causeway // Hours Different hours each day, so check website for opening times // Ages 3+

TIP: The Mall at Cribbs Causeway usually has a temporary ice rink at Christmas.

77_PLAY PADEL

It's Europe's fastest growing sport

Padel is easy to pick up, but difficult to master. It's not Europe's fastest growing sport for nothing, and since August 2022 we have been able to play it in Bristol, thanks to the city's first purpose-built courts from Padel4All: four floodlit courts in the grounds of Lockleaze Sports Centre.

The sport is played on indoor courts and is a cross between squash and tennis, with players able to hit the ball over the net with the help of see-through walls. If you've never played before: no problem! One-hour coach-led sessions will teach you how to hold the racket, and basic groundstrokes, volleys, overheads and serve; court positioning and where to stand; and the rules and how to score. By the end of a session, which costs just £5, you'll be competing like you've played padel your whole life.

One of the best things about this young sport is that it is always played in doubles, with two teams of two at either side of the net on the enclosed courts roughly 25 per cent smaller than the size of a tennis court. Padel is also known as 'padel tennis' and uses the same scoring system as tennis. A big difference, however, is that all serves are underarm – just one of the reasons it's so popular with beginners.

Padel4All has a burgeoning community and schools outreach programme in this area of north Bristol, as well as being fully accessible. At Padel4All's centre, you can hire or buy rackets and balls if you don't have your own, and chill out on sofas between the courts while you're not improving your skills.

Address Lockleaze Sports Centre, Bonnington Walk, Lockleaze, BS7 9XF, +44 (0)117 4051530, www.padel4all.com/lockleaze // Getting there Bus 24 to Bonnington Walk or cycle to Lockleaze via Concorde Way // Hours Mon–Fri 8am–10pm, Sat & Sun 8am–8pm // Ages 4+

TIP: Bristol Rovers Women's FC (the Gas Girls) play their home games at Lockleaze Sports Centre.

78_PLAYFULL TOYSHOP

Sustainably sourced wooden toys

The range of toys at Playfull Toyshop is best exemplified in a box in one corner where there is a selection of wooden swords. Take your pick from a heroic knight or Viking's broadsword, a Roman cavalry long sword, naval boarding cutlass, legionary's gladius and Poignard sword. Or just get a simple wooden dagger. On the floor nearby, bows and arrows are for sale in a wicker basket next to fishing nets.

Playfull specialises in sustainably sourced wooden toys, as well as books, puzzles, games and art kits. The story of the shop itself is good enough to feature in a book: Kerstin Price started making cloth dolls for her three children in the 1980s, continued making them for friends and family, and began selling them at school fairs. She then started importing hand-made wooden toys from her native Sweden before opening this toyshop on the fiercely independent Gloucester Road with her husband Nigel.

Walk into the carpeted back room, up a small step and find more books as well as craft materials and a bargain table, with rainbow beams coming from what looks like a piece of heart-shaped cut diamond in the window. Try out the pens on a book permanently on the table.

A few doors up Gloucester Road is another toy shop more than twice its size. Totally Toys is always on top of the latest trends, whether that is fidget spinners or thinking putty, with science and STEM products always big sellers. Make a volcano or make your own slime, or just ask very nicely for the latest Harry Potter or Star Wars Lego sets.

Address 87 Gloucester Road, Bishopston, BS7 8AS,
+44 (0)117 9446767, www.playfulltoyshop.com // Getting there
15-minute walk from Broadmead; bus 73 to Gloucester Road //
Hours Tue–Sat 10am–5pm // Ages 2+

TIP: Old-fashioned sweet shop Scrumptiously Sweet is at 83 Gloucester Road.

79__PUMP IT UP

Get on your bike

With changes to the plans for the new Western Harbour development close to Cumberland Basin at the time of writing, one feature of the current space is definitely set to be retained when the site is developed for hundreds of new homes sometime in the future. It's the pump track, well hidden beneath the elevated road system, and somewhere your legs, gravity and momentum propel you forwards rather than the internal combustion engine in the cars zooming on Brunel Way above.

Bristol's newest pump track in Stockwood was officially opened in May 2022 by Olympic freestyle BMX bronze medallist, Declan Brooks. The sensational new cycling facility was constructed by specialist south Bristol-based track builders Velosolutions, and features their signature red go-faster stripes. The new facility is part of a cycling inclusion programme from charity Access Sport, which aims to give every young person access to a bike, the skills and confidence to use it, and somewhere local, safe and exciting to enjoy riding. The open-access facility is accessible for bikes, scooters and skateboards, with a storage unit providing a safe place to store community bikes and helmets.

The beauty of pump tracks – with others in Hartcliffe, Hillfields and Arnos Park – is that they are both playground and training facilities. Practise the basic skills, and as you get better there will be more of a challenge with an increase in speed and skill.

Address Brunel Way Pump Track, Brunel Way, BS3 2LE; Stockwood Bike Park, Whittock Road, Stockwood, BS14 8DE, www.facebook.com/StockwoodBikeHub // Getting there Underneath Brunel Way; bus 2 to Sturminster Road // Hours Accessible 24 hours // Ages 4+

TIP: Mud Dock in the city centre is both a cycle shop and café.

80_PURDOWN PERCY

Rumours, myths and local legend

Some people think it's a refuelling point for UFOs. There is even a rumour that a nearby copse of trees spells out the letter 'B' to make it easier for aliens to land here on their intergalactic adventures. (If you enjoy rumours, listen out for the 'Bristol hum' and look up the story of the parking attendant at the former Bristol Zoo in Clifton.)

The distinctive tower on a hill called Purdown in Stoke Park is one of Bristol's best known modern landmarks. It's actually a telecommunications tower built by BT in 1970, and now ensures that mobile phones can work. At the top of Purdown, you can get an amazing panoramic view across much of the city and onto the countryside beyond. You can walk to almost underneath the tower, with the land inhabited by a small herd of goats, whose main job is to graze the scrub that has grown up here.

Much of the scrub is around the solid concrete remains of an anti-aircraft gun battery built during World War II in an attempt to shoot down enemy bombers before they could drop their deadly cargo. These guns were incredibly loud, and a local legend sprang up that there was a 'supergun' here – given the name of Purdown Percy.

It was just a rumour, that might have started due to the enormous sound of the guns or that they were able to fire simultaneously. They may have been loud, but they were not very successful, with only two of the hundreds of German bombers flying over Bristol between 1939 and 1945 shot down by the city's anti-aircraft guns.

TIP: Boing! softplay family centre is on nearby Gainsborough Square in Lockleaze.

Address Purdown, Stoke Park, BS7 9UP //
Getting there Bus 24 to Romney Avenue //
Hours Accessible 24 hours // Ages 2+

81_RAINBOW CROSSING

Celebrating the city's LGBTQ+ community

Bristol's first and only rainbow crossing was repainted ahead of the city's Pride celebrations in 2022, which saw the annual parade make its way through the city centre for the first time in three years ahead of a huge party on the Downs. Pride is all about shining a light on Bristol's LGBTQ+ community, and the rainbow crossing on Wine Street is a striking visual representation of their diversity.

After fading in the years since it was first painted, the colours making up the Pride Progress flag were reapplied in harder wearing paint to show Bristol's support for its lesbian, gay, bisexual and transgender community. The crossing was first painted in 2020 as a call for equality and to give visibility to the community at a time when the pandemic stopped many events taking place. Its repainting two years later came in the year that marked 50 years since the UK's first-ever Pride march.

Bristol's rainbow crossing is the focal point along Bristol's Pride march, where thousands of people from community groups, charities, public sector organisations and businesses join forces to support LGBTQ+ human rights. But the march is just one within almost a month-long series of events, which in 2022 saw film screenings, exhibitions, a football festival in partnership with the Gas Girls and even a dog show.

Remember that Pride is also a protest: amplifying, maintaining and furthering LGBTQ+ human rights. It's about celebrating community and showing that hatred and prejudice have no place in Bristol or anywhere else.

TIP: Find some peace in the Castle Park Physic Garden to the side of St Peter's Church.

Address Wine Street, BS1 2DD // Getting there The crossing is between the top of Union Street and Castle Park // Hours Accessible 24 hours // Ages 3+

82_RED LODGE

From partying to girls' education

In 2010, a secret well was discovered under the floor of one room within the Red Lodge. Nobody knew that it had existed, as it had been bricked over and covered with stone flagstones, and later with a wooden floor. Further investigations showed that it was just over 40 feet deep, and dendrochronology (the study of growth rings in trees) confirmed that it dated from the 16th century. The well had probably been dug by Elizabethan workers at the same time as the Red Lodge was constructed in 1580, when it would have been outside the building.

The Red Lodge's first use was as a place for partying for Sir John Young and his wife Dame Joan who lived in a grand house on the site of what is now Bristol Beacon. The Great Oak Room on the first floor is the last complete Elizabethan room in Bristol, with the top craftsmen of the day spending two years carving the oak, sculpting the stone and moulding the ceiling. Look at the elaborate plasterwork of the ceiling in the bedroom next door, which inspired the design of the garden, and which can also be best seen from this room.

TIP: Find an eclectic variety of independent shops on Colston Street.

Over the subsequent centuries, the Red Lodge became a home, passing through many different families, before in 1854 becoming the UK's and possibly the world's first reformatory school for girls. Its aim was to give underprivileged girls an education, rather than leave them to the more traditional Victorian methods that often saw some of the poorest and most deprived children at the time sent to prison or the workhouse.

Address Park Row, BS1 5LJ, +44 (0)117 9211360, www.bristolmuseums.org.uk/red-lodge-museum // Getting there Short walk from top of Christmas Steps // Hours Apr–Oct Mon, Tue, Sat & Sun 11am–4pm // Ages 3+

83_ RIDE ON
A FIREFIGHTING BOAT

Especially made for Bristol's docks

Be prepared to get wet if you take a ride on *Pyronaut*. This boat was built to fight fires in Bristol's once busy docks, when huge industrial buildings used to overlook the harbour and the fastest way to reach them was by water. It no longer fights fires, but its cannons still work, and they are fired (pun well and truly intended) on regular rides, drawing water out of the harbour and, if the wind is blowing in the right direction, coming straight back down on you sitting in the boat!

Sitting in the boat with you will be volunteers who perhaps might include Clive, who was a member of the crew on *Pyronaut* when the boat was in service, and will regale you with tales from his firefighting days. *Pyronaut* was made especially for Bristol's docks and is low enough to fit under the city's numerous bridges (see ch. 11). It served from 1934 until 1973 and worked particularly hard in the Blitz from 1940 to 1941. With countless warehouses, factories, shops and homes around the harbour damaged during this time, *Pyronaut* was constantly manned and worked through some of the worst bombing raids of the war.

Pyronaut is not the only storeyed boat that you can take rides on in the docks. There is the little steam tug *Mayflower*, the oldest steam tug in the world, which was built in Bristol in 1861 and worked on the ship canal between Sharpness and Gloucester for over a century. And there is also the *John King*, a 1935 diesel tug built to tow cargo ships from the centre of Bristol to the mouth of the River Avon.

TIP: Bookhaus on Rope Walk behind M Shed is a brilliant bookshop.

Address M Shed, Princes Wharf, Wapping Road, BS1 4RN, www.bristolmuseums.org.uk/m-shed/whats-on/pyronaut-trips // Getting there Buy tickets from the ticket office by the M Shed railway platform close to Prince Street; short walk from M Shed or from Prince Street bridge // Hours Check website for timetable // Ages 3+

84_ROMAN REMAINS

Marooned in the middle of a housing estate

The honest truth is that you're better off making the short trip to our neighbouring city if you want to understand more about the time when Romans lived in these parts. Unlike Bath, there was no major Roman settlement in Bristol. Bath's Roman baths right in the centre of the city feature costumed characters and an audioguide, designed just for children, read by Michael Rosen.

But bear with us! Because marooned in the middle of a housing estate in north Bristol is a villa that was once the home of a wealthy Roman family, and can now be accessed by borrowing a key from nearby Blaise Castle Museum. The villa, which features the only Roman bath suite in Bristol and original mosaic floors, was discovered during the construction of the Lawrence Weston estate in 1947.

In the Roman period, the major Roman settlement in the Bristol area was Abona – on a bend of the River Avon, where Sea Mills is located today. Abona was linked to Bath by a Roman road whose remains can still be seen on the Downs between Stoke Bishop and Clifton.

The villa at Kings Weston was a mile away from Abona, and thanks to coins found there has been dated to the end of the third century. It is likely that it was once at the centre of a villa estate, with the family living in it controlling satellite rural settlements. Its demise came around A.D. 367 with the west wing burnt down, probably by Irish raiders. Your own raid on the villa today will allow you to see where Romans once lived in Bristol and even discover Roman central heating!

Address Long Cross, Lawrence Weston, BS11 0LP // Getting there Bus 4 to Long Cross // Hours Visible from the road; unescorted visits to the site may be made by picking up a key from Blaise Museum or Bristol Museum no later than 2pm // Ages 5+

85_ST NICHOLAS MARKET

A treasure trove of delights

Are you even from Bristol or have you even paid a visit to the city if you do not own at least one item of clothing from Beast? Head to their stall in St Nicholas Market – better known as St Nick's – to find t-shirts, socks and babygrows, many with popular Bristolian refrains such as 'Cheers drive' (Thank you, bus driver), 'Gert lush' (very good) and 'Alright my luvver?' (How are you?). Beast also has a number of other items for sale that make perfect gifts and souvenirs including mugs, magnets and pin badges.

Beast can be found in the middle of the Exchange Hall section of the market alongside other stalls selling – deep breath – toys, jewellery, hats, incense, candles, fossils, hot sauce, hats, vintage kimonos, wallets, lamps and stamps. See if you can find one item for sale starting with every letter of the alphabet. The loser gets a wooden spoon (they are, of course, for sale as well).

Hungry? Grab a roll from Royce Rolls who have been here since 1979 or a chicken curry from Spice Up Your Life, or head to the Glass Arcade for some of the best food options in Bristol. The A to Z can now be done with food, from Matina's naan bread to Pieminister's pies, Portuguese custard tarts to Caribbean wraps, couscous to churros. Thirsty? Try a smoothie from Big Juice.

> TIP: Four bronze pedestals on Corn Street are known as 'nails' and date back to Elizabethan times.

Continue walking through St Nick's and you'll come to the Covered Market. Watch musical instruments be repaired through the window of Studio 7, explore South Africa without leaving Kalahari Moon, choose delicious sweets from old-fashioned glass jars in Treasure Island and buy a second-hand book from Beware of the Leopard.

Address Corn Street, BS1 1JQ.
www.bristol.gov.uk/web/st-nicholas-markets //
Getting there 5-minute walk from fountains //
Hours Mon–Sat 9.30am–5pm // Ages 4+

86_ ST PAUL'S ADVENTURE PLAYGROUND

Play to your heart's content

A huge tree-trunk forms the centrepiece of St Paul's Adventure Playground, on top of which is a circular room that looks as if it is made out of a stained-glass window. From here extend ladders, ropes and netting. Try to make your way around the edge of the site without touching the ground as more trees provide support for wooden walkways, or become Tarzan and swing on ropes overlooking not the jungle but the M32 – from which many people might have seen this playground but never visited. Well, what are you waiting for!

'All adults must be accompanied by a child' reads one hand-painted sign. For older children, on another corner of the site is a basketball court. For smaller children or those with less daredevil tendencies, there are ever-changing craft activities. Come one day and make collages, another day and paint murals. And for those who need it, food is served for free.

There was an inspirational outpouring of support for the playground in 2020 following a devastating arson attack. A crowdfunding campaign raised almost £36,000 to help rebuild after the fire. Also raising much-needed money for this much-loved community asset is Children's Bicycle Exchange, a bike workshop located to one side of the playground, offering refurbished child and adult bikes, as well as services and repairs.

TIP: Don't miss the annual St Paul's Carnival, which takes place on the first Saturday of July.

If you like what you find at St Paul's Adventure Playground, find similarly adventurous places across Bristol including Felix Road Adventure Playground in Easton, The Ranch in Southmead and The Vench in Lockleaze.

Address Fern Street, St Paul's, BS2 9LN,
www.apeproject.co.uk // Getting there
10-minute walk from Cabot Circus //
Hours Thu & Fri 3.15 – 6.15pm,
Sat 10am – noon & 1 – 5pm // Ages 5+

87_ SCRIBBLE & SKETCH

For petit Picassos and miniature Monets

The Royal West of England Academy – more commonly known as the RWA – is one of Bristol's most august organisations. No, not that August. We're not talking about the month between July and September but 'having great importance and respect in society' (thanks, Cambridge Dictionary!). Located in a Grade II*-listed building that reopened in 2022 after a £4.5m refurbishment, the RWA's patron is His Majesty King Charles III, and works by many world-famous artists have been on display here – as well as watercolours by the King painted while he was still the Prince of Wales. This was Bristol's first art gallery and is still its most prestigious.

One aspect of the recent transformation is to make the RWA a little less fuddy-duddy. And Scribble & Sketch sessions are the perfect example of that – with the free monthly family art workshops not just taking place at the gallery but also at Hartcliffe Children's Centre, Easton Community Centre, Faithspace in Redcliffe and the Greenway Centre in Southmead. The sessions are designed for children and adults to take part in together, and led by an artist sharing a variety of different techniques.

Look out for other child-friendly activities at the RWA, including Junior Drawing School for kids aged 5+; and Bring Your Baby tours, where parents do not have to worry about their babies making a noise in the galleries.

You can also head to the RWA website to download some Scribble & Sketch workshops for home, with themes including silhouettes, leaf printing and Diwali cards.

Address RWA, Queen's Road, Clifton, BS8 1PX, +44 (0)117 9735129, www.rwa.org.uk/products/scribble-and-sketch // Getting there 4-minute walk from top of Park Street // Hours At RWA, first Sat of month 10.30am–12.30pm; check website for times at other locations // Ages 1+

TIP: Spike Island art gallery on Cumberland Road used to be a tea packing factory.

88_SEAGULL STREET ART

A two-winged vandal

We all love to play hide and seek, right? But have you ever played hide and seek with a giant seagull? No? Well here is your chance! Despite the bird being the size of a three-storey building, she still takes a bit of looking for. Let me give you a few clues: walk down North Street away from the Tobacco Factory towards Greville Smyth Park. Go past Aldi and past Ashton Gate Primary School. Keep your eyes open! Have you found her yet?

There she is! With her head peeking out, looking down North Street from Back Road. It's not the best hiding spot, and the bird won't get any points for camouflage; but cut her some slack: her wingspan is probably the size of a few houses and it's not as if she can move, because she is not made of feathers but of paint.

The seagull street art was painted by east London-based street artists Irony and Boe in 2018 for Upfest, Bristol's colourful annual celebration of street art. The duo enjoy creating art not just *in* locations, but art *of* the locations in which they find themselves, including here in south Bristol.

The elusive pair have a habit of painting birds, with other work including two pigeons further up North Street from this suspicious seagull above the Hen & Chicken. Away from creatures of the feathered variety is a veritable menagerie of mammals: a cow, mouse, cat, fox, dog, squirrel, stag and even a claw-loving three-eyed green alien from *Toy Story* – which I'm not sure can be officially counted as a mammal but is probably a perfect companion for hide and seek.

> TIP: Greville Smyth Park has a playground suitable for both younger and older children.

Address Back Road, Bedminster, BS3 1JU // Getting there 2-minute walk from Tobacco Factory, 1-minute walk from Greville Smyth Park // Hours Accessible 24 hours // Ages 2+

89_ SKATE – IN A POOL

Skating has replaced splashing

If you want to practise your heelflips, ollies and grinds, then one of the best places in Bristol is somewhere that used to see dives, crawls and splashes. Because this purpose-built indoor concrete skatepark is inside a disused swimming pool that has a brilliant new second life as a world-class street-based park. You can buy new kit in a shop or chill out in the on-site café.

cool

If you're new to skating, then Campus Pool is ideal for beginners, hosting a wide range of events for different age groups, all abilities and disciplines, from newbies to wannabe pros, as well as girls-only sessions. And it's not just skateboarding here but scooting as well as balance bikes during the toddler-takeovers. Hone your skills in one-to-one or group sessions, or book into Skate Club every school holiday, which sees a day of play and learning.

Campus' founders set out to use skateboarding as a tool to engage with children and young people, opening this space in 2015. It retains many of the features of the old swimming pool that it was until the 1970s, making for a quirky and original space. Among the concrete ramps are tiles that swimmers used to push off from that are now jumped over using tricks that can be glimpsed from a viewing gallery that doubles up as the shop.

A recent successful crowdfunder has seen the building of a new mini ramp and beginners' section, made out of high impact birch ply, a little bit more forgiving than the concrete in the main section. Because even the best skaters will always fall over!

Address Whitchurch Lane, Bishopsworth, BS13 7RW, +44 (0)117 9641178, www.campusskateparks.co.uk/pages/pool // Getting there Cycle with your skateboard on your back along the Malago Greenway, or catch the 75 bus to Church Road // Hours Sat, Sun & Tue 10am–6pm, Wed–Fri 10am–9pm // Ages 2+

90_SKYBOAT CAFÉ

A community hub for young families

You can easily get distracted by the food and drink at Skyboat Café before you even make it into the cut-above-the-rest soft play area, accessed through a small gate with the push of a button. The gate is to stop tiny punters from escaping. But why would they? This is one of the best places in town for pre-schoolers and their grown-ups.

Skyboat is run by two local mums, Lara and Stef, whose original aim was to create a place where adults would want to go for coffee and meet up with friends, and know that their kids would also be able to play and have a great time. It has swiftly become a community hub for young families, a place to make new friends, and a support network for new parents. With a background in Michelin-starred restaurants, it's Stef who is responsible for the food. Expect to find a counter groaning with delicious cakes, with the likes of shakshuka and salads on the healthy lunchtime menu; and a mouthwatering children's selection including buttermilk pancakes, sweet potato waffles and smashed avocado toast fingers.

Take your shoes off and walk through the gate to find an area for babies with a lava-lamp-like tube in one corner in ever-changing colours, and a padded area in muted shades. The next room along in the Tardis-like space, which used to be a furniture shop, is for toddlers, and features a multi-layered place to explore featuring tunnels, slides and netting. The back room is used for weekly workshops including mum and baby yoga, pregnancy yoga, and baby massage.

> TIP: Redland Green is a great park to run around in.

Address 4 Harcourt Road, Redland, BS6 7RG, www.skyboatcafe.com // Getting there Bus 505 to Westbury Park; 15-minute walk from Whiteladies Road // Hours Tue–Fri 9am–3.30pm // Ages 3 months+

91_SLIDEY ROCK

A site of special slidentific interest

Nobody knows who was the first person to slide down the slidey rock, known alternatively as the slippy rock, the rock slide, the bum slide, the Clifton slide or simply just the slider. But whoever it was deserves to be in the history books as a true trail-blazer, because the slidey rock has since become a much-loved feature of our city, worn smooth by generations of Bristolian bottoms.

Climb confidently over the fences at the top near Observatory Hill – once home to an Iron Age fort, so children could have been sliding here for thousands of years – take your marks and go! You will probably slide faster than you expect, especially nearer the end, so take heed. Across Bristol, people have stories of bruises, bumps and scrapes, and friction burns on delicate areas of the anatomy.

Want more names for the feature that we are calling the slidey rock after a highly unscientific Twitter poll? *Swallows and Amazons* fans might call it the 'knickerbockerbreaker' after a rocky waterfall discovered by the Swallows in the book *Swallowdale* by Arthur Ransome. Some people call it the donkey slide for reasons lost in the mists of time. Spanish speakers may call it the 'chorraera'. And if we're going to get technical, it's an anthropogenically polished carboniferous limestone escarpment.

One of the greatest joys of the slidey rock is being able to introduce young sliders to something that has been passed down through the generations. Whatever you call it, the slidey rock is a Bristolian rite of passage.

Address Between Clifton Suspension Bridge and Clifton Observatory, Litfield Place, BS8 3LT // **Getting there** Walk along the path that starts close to the junction of Observatory Road and Sion Hill; find the slidey rock before you reach Observatory Hill // **Hours** Accessible 24 hours // **Ages** 6+

TIP: The nearby Suspension Bridge playground has a good selection of mostly wooden play equipment.

92__ SNUFF MILLS

The countryside in the city

One of the greatest joys of Bristol is that there are swathes of countryside in the middle of the city. An example of this is Snuff Mills, just a few hundred yards from the M32, but a verdant oasis perfectly made for exploring. Choose to take the high path, the low path or the middle path, following the course of the River Frome through a woodland valley.

There were once five mills in this valley, with just one remaining. Look closely and you can still see its huge waterwheel. Industry also included quarrying, with Pennant sandstone from here used for many buildings across Bristol, as well as for kerb stones that we walk over every day.

TIP: Pick your own veg and buy wildflowers at Grow Wilder on Frenchay Park Road.

Join a ragtag collection of walkers, runners and cyclists in Snuff Mills. Walk off the main paths, up steep steps or winding tracks, to find examples of what was here in the olden days: gate posts, tumbledown stone walls and telltale signs of those long-gone mills. Or climb up and down slopes to find a world of tangled tree roots. Don't forget your wellies if you want to do some splashing or dip your fishing net into the river.

Your reward, if you follow the path eastwards, will be Oldbury Court Estate, which has a new play area with a water and sand play zone, and a pirate play ship for younger children; and a rope bridge and zip wire for older children. Or follow the Frome Valley Walkway westwards to Eastville Park, which also has a popular play area as well as a lake, tennis courts and an old swimming pool now often used for outdoor theatre productions, with a parkrun taking place every Saturday morning.

Address River View, Stapleton, BS16 1DL // Getting there Bus 48A to Broom Hill // Hours Accessible 24 hours // Ages 3+

93_STREET ART SELFIES

The original face masks

Bristol is world renowned for its street art, with the work of home-grown talent able to be appreciated across the city. Banksy is the most well-known exponent of the craft, but look out also for work on walls across the city from Acerone, Andy Council, Cheo and Inkie, to name just four. And the traditionally male-dominated scene is also now being countered by the likes of the Women In Paint Collective, who host monthly paint jams and provide support and advice for women painting outside.

Bristol's global reputation draws global street art talent, one of whom does not paint on walls but rather leaves his face attached to them. A street art selfie if you will. A face mask before the pandemic made them ubiquitous. The artist's name is Gregos, who lives in Paris but whose work can be found – if you know where to look – in cities around Europe.

In his native France, Gregos is known as *le passe-muraille*: the man who walks through walls. A visit to Greek temples had a profound effect on him, and when he returned to Paris, he began learning different sculpture techniques, making imprints of his hands and face. His masks soon became reflections of his mood, 'drawing inspiration from his surroundings, current events, life and the street… (he) never tires of using his medium like a mirror for sharing emotions,' according to his website.

Find his playful work glued onto the right-hand side of Bristol Bridge as you walk away from Baldwin Street and on Small Street close to the entrance to Leonard Lane.

Address Small Street: next to entrance to Leonard Lane opposite Betties & Baldwins, BS1 1DB; Bristol Bridge on Welsh Back side // Getting there Both pieces are a few minutes' walk from St Nick's Market // Hours Accessible 24 hours // Ages 4+

TIP: Just imagine when Bristol Bridge was lined with buildings five storeys high. It even had a large chapel that formed a central gatehouse.

94_TOOTBUS

A circular tour of the city

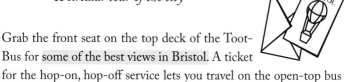

Grab the front seat on the top deck of the Toot-Bus for some of the best views in Bristol. A ticket for the hop-on, hop-off service lets you travel on the open-top bus as many times as you want over a 48-hour period, so you can ride around Bristol's streets to your heart's content. (And before you start sniggering at the back, Toot is an acronym for The Original Open Top Tour. How did you even think it could mean anything else?)

Go sightseeing around the centre, up Park Street, along Whiteladies Road and up Blackboy Hill, skirt the Downs via the former home of Bristol Zoo, head into Clifton Village, go down Bridge Valley Road and underneath the Clifton Suspension Bridge (time to get your camera out!), into Hotwells for a view of the SS *Great Britain* the other side of the Floating Harbour, up Baldwin Street and across Bristol Bridge, towards Temple Meads via Victoria Street, along Redcliffe Way by St Mary Redcliffe church and back to the start. There are 14 stops along the way, with an audioguide to listen to via headphones.

While we're here, let's clear up some confusion around Whiteladies Road and Blackboy Hill. Contrary to rumour, they almost certainly have no association with slavery. The name Whiteladies Road is most likely to have come from Whiteladies House, itself named after white ladies, otherwise known as snowdrops. Blackboy Hill meanwhile is probably named after a pub that once stood here, named after King Charles II who was also known as the Black Boy because of his swarthy complexion.

Address Start and finish on Broad Quay, www.tootbus.com // Getting there Short walk from fountains or from Queen Square // Hours Apr–Oct 10am–4pm // Ages 2+

TIP: The Harbourside Street Food Market takes place by the fountains every Wed, Thu, Sat and Sun.

95_TREASURE ISLAND TRAIL

Follow in the footsteps of fearsome pirates

If you love reading, you've probably visited Bristol before. J. K. Rowling was born in Yate, on the outskirts of our city, and local links are present in the *Harry Potter* series if you look hard enough. For example, the Dursley family were named after the Gloucestershire town of the same name. And on his way to them as a baby with Hagrid, young Harry fell asleep while the pair were flying over Bristol.

Back to ground level, and we need to swap witches and wizards for the skull and crossbones as we raise the Jolly Roger for a journey into Bristol's piratical past. The most famous pirate who ever sailed the seven seas was born in Bristol in 1680. Edward Teach changed his name to Blackbeard when he commanded a gang some 400-strong, sailing in former slave ship *Queen Anne's Revenge*, and stuffing smoking fuses in his hair to frighten his enemies.

Bristol's links with Robert Louis Stevenson's classic novel, *Treasure Island*, are marked on a series of barrels that form a self-guided walking tour. The Treasure Island Trail retells significant events in the book. For example, Long John Silver is landlord of the Spyglass Inn, which is based on the Hole In The Wall pub on one corner of Queen Square.

TIP: Find a new book at indies including Bookhaus, Gloucester Road Books, Good Book Shop, Heron Books, Max Minerva's, Small City Bookshop and Storysmith.

The trail lasts around one hour, with theatre company Show of Strength (www.showofstrength.org.uk) organising regular walks following the trail during the school holidays. Be prepared for terrible pirate jokes and Ted, the fact-checking parrot, to make sure your pirate gets their story straight. Shiver me timbers!

Treasure Island Trail
What I Heard in the
Apple Barrel

Redcliffe Wharf

Address Start the trail outside
Merchant Venturers' Almshouses,
King Street, BS1 4DT,
www.longjohnsilvertrust.co.uk //
Getting there Short walk from
fountains or from Bristol Old Vic //
Hours Accessible 24 hours // Ages 4+

96_TWENTIETH CENTURY FLICKS

Bristol's smallest cinema

Have you always wanted to watch your favourite film at the cinema? Twentieth Century Flicks allows you to hire a screen for you and your friends and family so you can create your own movie magic. Birthday parties are a particular favourite here within Bristol's last video shop – and quite possibly the longest running video rental store in the world – which has survived the transitions from VHS to DVD to streaming, and now has more than 20,000 titles to take home, as well as two cinema screens to hire.

Flicks' two screens are the Videodrome, which seats 18 people, and the Kino with a capacity of eight people. You really can choose any film you want and take a seat on chairs rescued from old cinema auditoriums. The only caveat is that under-18s need to be accompanied by at least one adult.

To make your cinema experience even more authentic, the shop sells popcorn, crisps, chocolate and fizzy drinks, and you can make as much noise as you want, even if you have already seen your favourite film 100 times before and know all of the words! So turn off the lights, sit back and relax. This is your time.

In 2022, Twentieth Century Flicks celebrated its 40th birthday by hosting the Forbidden Worlds film festival in the former IMAX cinema next to Bristol Aquarium (see ch. 12). The festival only screened movies from 1982, including children's favourites *The Dark Crystal* and *The Secret of NIMH*. Keep a look out for the festival dedicated to screening films from around the world and celebrating the people who made them.

Address 19 Christmas Steps, BS1 5BS, +44 (0)117 9258432, www.20thcenturyflicks.co.uk // Getting there 5-minute walk from fountains // Hours Variable (check website for details) // Ages 4+

TIP: Christmas Steps (not actually steps at all) is named after a chapel dedicated to the Three Wise Men at the top.

97_THE TWO MINUTE HAND CLOCK

It's time for Bristol Time

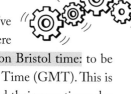

If you're ever late for anything in Bristol, you've got an extremely valid excuse. Arrive anywhere around 10 minutes late and you're running on Bristol time: to be precise, 11 minutes behind Greenwich Mean Time (GMT). This is a throwback to when places across the UK had their own times depending on when the Sun rose and set. This changed with the growing railway network needing standardised hours for their timetables, but one clock in Bristol is a reminder of those, umm, times.

Look up at the clock above the Exchange building, now the main entrance to St Nick's Market (see ch. 85) and you will see three hands. One of these is the hour hand: nothing unusual with that. But you will also see one minute hand in black and one minute hand in red. The black minute hand is Bristol time, and it remains here because of the belligerence of Bristolians that continues to this day. Because we didn't want this newfangled time imposed on us from that there London, and kept Bristol time for several years after it was adopted in the rest of the UK.

Bristol is full of fascinating clocks. As well as this one on Corn Street, another interesting timepiece is on College Green on the side of what is now Costa, which was the city's 'master clock' when GMT was introduced nationwide by law in 1847. And the blue clock on St Augustine's Parade was originally on the side of the former Bristol Tramways office, with the Tramways Centre tram stop remembered in the name of the area that everyone still calls 'the centre'.

Address The Exchange, Corn Street, BS1 1JQ // Getting there Short walk from St Nick's Market or 4-minute walk from fountains // Hours Accessible 24 hours // Ages 3+

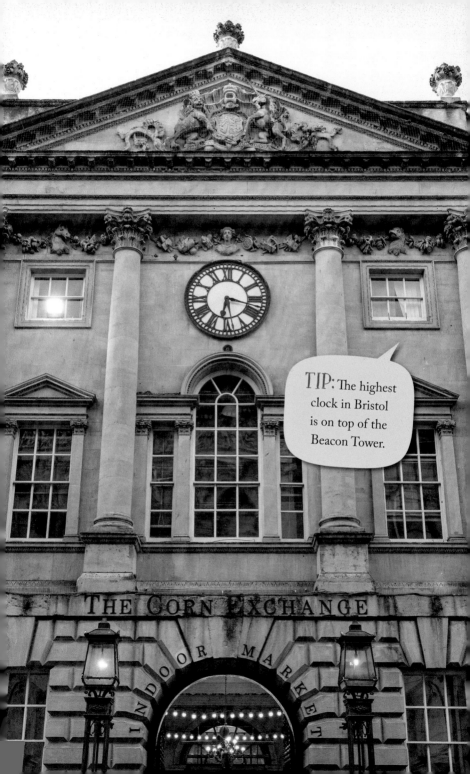

98_AN UNDERGROUND FOOTPATH

Not even on some maps

A tunnel forming a section of a public footpath is one of Bristol's most unusual listed structures. Okay, it's not exactly a secret to everyone – the tunnel is in fact Grade II-listed – but because of its location it remains remarkably well hidden. The underground passageway is not on Google Maps and is not signposted, even from the churchyard in which it begins.

The tunnel is located underneath the garden of an old vicarage, known as Rectory Gardens, with a short section of it open to the elements. It forms part of a footpath heading from one corner of the churchyard of St Mary's in Henbury to Blaise Castle, crossing over a small stone bridge over Hazel Brook. On the Know Your Place website, the subterranean thoroughfare is marked as a 'post-medieval tunnel'. But on its Historic England listing, it is dated from around 1835 and made with 'rubble, brick arches, copper-slag block coping and Pennant steps. Tunnel with segmental-arched roof, reached by steps down from the churchyard. Built to carry a public footpath below the rear yard of The Old Vicarage.'

St Mary's Church was probably founded in the late seventh century, with parts of the current church dating from around 1200. Two interesting features of its churchyard – close to where the footpath starts – are the grave of an enslaved child Scipio Africanus, who died in 1720, with an elaborately painted headstone and footstone featuring black cherubs; and an obelisk at the grave of the author-turned-Egyptologist Amelia Edwards, who died in 1892.

TIP: Bristol doesn't have an underground railway network but mayor Marvin Rees wants to build one!

Address Church Close, Henbury,
BS10 7QF // Getting there Bus 1
to Crow Lane, Henbury // Hours
Accessible 24 hours // Ages 4+

99_UPSIDE-DOWN FISH

A fish diving into a pond in Fishponds

On the site of the old Fishponds station along the route of the Bristol & Bath Railway Path, an inverted fish made of bricks dives down into a pond. A time capsule collected by local children is concreted in its belly, with the sculpture's bricks recently given a lick of paint.

(By the way, yes, there is a place in Bristol called Fishponds! It takes its name from some ponds that were once located here, made from empty quarries, with many miners and quarrymen who dug for coal and pennant stone once living in the village.)

While cycling along the Bristol & Bath Railway Path, you can't miss this fish. It also acts as a milestone for your onward journey: three miles to Bristol and 12 miles to Bath. If you reach Bath and don't fancy the cycle ride back to Bristol, just jump on the train.

The Railway Path, also just known as the Path, was the very first section of the National Cycle Network to be built by Bristol-based sustainable transport charity Sustrans. It has been claimed that the 10,000-mile web of car-free routes is the longest outdoor gallery in the world.

Sustrans commissioned artist Doug Cocker to create this sculpture, called *Fish on its Nose,* in 1993. It was built by bricklaying apprentices from house builder Wimpey. Look out for other artwork

on the Path, including a centurion near Warmley marking the crossing of a Roman road. In March 2022, a year-long creative project also began at the ruins of Mangotsfield station near Fishponds, with five new artist commissions.

Address Close to the junction of Hockey's Lane and New Station Way, Fishponds, BS16 3LD // Getting there Cycle along the Bristol & Bath Railway Path, or 2-minute walk from Fishponds Road; bus 48, 49 or Y5 // Hours Accessible 24 hours // Ages 3+

TIP: Mi Café Su Café serves food and drink from a converted Citroën van close to the sculpture.

100_ WAKE THE TIGER

The world's first 'amazement park'

How to describe Wake The Tiger? It's actually best not to know too much. To arrive with as little prior knowledge as possible about what its creators – the same people behind Boomtown festival – have dubbed the world's first 'amazement park'.

After her first visit, a seven-year-old described Wake The Tiger as 'mysterious' and then politely demanded that her father take her around twice again in case they had missed anything. Which they had. Loads! Look everywhere for secret passageways, hidden clues and a friend from school who you might bump into behind a bookshelf that's actually a hidden door if you find the right book.

 Before Wake The Tiger opened in 2022, creative director Lak Mitchell told the Bristol24/7 Behind the Headlines podcast that the best way to describe it is 'somewhere between an art gallery, a theme park and a film set'. 'From an aesthetic perspective, it sits somewhere between Mad Max, Willy Wonka and Harry Potter,' he added. 'We don't want to give things away. But at the same time, I don't really care. Because actually, there's no way that you can explain what is here until you come.'

So, without giving too much away, a visit here is a visit to an immersive art experience consisting of dozens of different creative environments including installations, soundscapes and those aforementioned secret passageways. Your journey will incongruously begin in the marketing suite of a luxury homes development, before an ancient tree becomes a portal between parallel worlds.

Address 127 Albert Road, St Philip's Marsh, BS2 0YA, www.wakethetiger.com // **Getting there** 15-minute walk from Bristol Temple Meads // **Hours** Wed & Thu noon–8pm, Fri noon–10pm, Sat 10am–10pm, Sun 10am–6pm // **Ages** 5+

TIP: Walk or cycle along St Philip's Greenway to find the bridge to nowhere.

101_ WALLED CITY WALK

Fallen former fortifications

Stand inside the central gateway of St John on the Wall church and you will be standing on the last remaining section of Bristol's city wall. Look up to see evidence of a portcullis that was once here close to a river that now runs underground. The name of the church is a clue to its original location as part of the wall. It was one of the main entrances and exits to the city, where travellers would pray, and some make generous donations before a journey.

Draw a circle around the intersection of Corn Street, Broad Street, High Street and Wine Street to see the area that 800 years ago was encircled by a wall made out of stone quarried from Brandon Hill. Bristol was one of England's three biggest towns in the 14th and 15th centuries, with the population living and often working in timber-framed houses built on top of extensive vaulted cellars. The growing city outgrew its Norman walls, but despite the walls no longer being visible (other than St John) it's still possible to follow some of their route.

In the Old City, much of the building and rebuilding over the centuries has respected the wall's original course. With your back to St John on the Wall and looking along Broad Street, turn right along Bell Lane and onto Leonard Lane, where steps lead down through what was once the wall onto St Stephen's Street. Or turn left along Tower Lane where you can imagine what it would have been like entering the medieval city through a passageway onto John Street, a modern recreation of an ancient entrance into Bristol.

Address The wall follows the route of Tower Lane, Bell Lane and Leonard Lane; download the Walled City Walk plan: www.bristololdcity.co.uk/old-city-heritage-trail // Getting there 5-minute walk from fountains // Hours Accessible 24 hours // Ages 4+

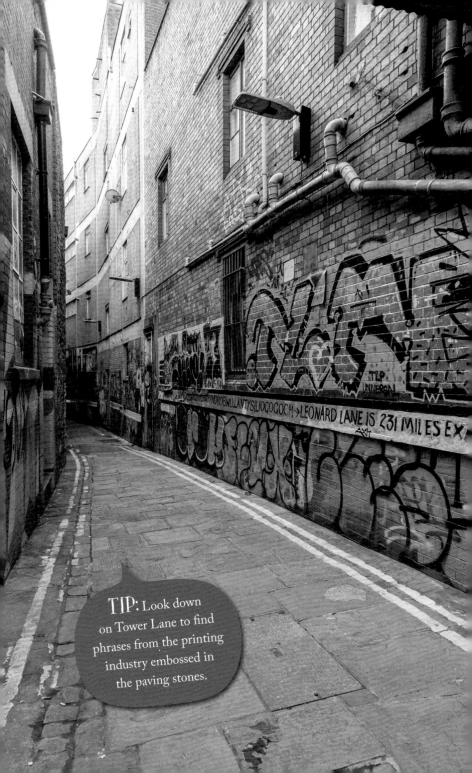

TIP: Look down on Tower Lane to find phrases from the printing industry embossed in the paving stones.

102_THE WAVE

Surf's up!

'Why do people surf?' asked a coach at a recent beginners' surf lesson at The Wave. Is it to have fun? Is it to keep fit? No! It's to look cool. At your first lesson, you will jump up and stand on the board on dry land, mastering the basics before taking to the water. Try not to think too much about it, but the way that you first stand on the board will be the way you surf for the rest of your life: either regular (left foot forward) or goofy (right foot forward).

The Wave is a very special place. It is the first inland surfing lake in the world using an extremely clever bit of technology that creates wave after perfect wave. So, unlike going to the beach and finding the sea as flat as a pancake, at The Wave there are ideal conditions guaranteed every single day. Splash around in the shallows with a bodyboard at the Play in the Bay sessions, learn the tricks of the trade from expert coaches, surf to your heart's content, or just chill out – with the sound of the waves washing over you.

For smaller children who might not yet be ready for surfing, there is a surf-themed outdoor play area and indoor craft activities. The on-site café-restaurant also has kids' meals, or you can bring your own food and drink.

If one day at The Wave is not enough, you can stay in The Camp. This is a collection of luxury tents with log-burning fires, enough room for six people to sleep, and, of course, space to store your surfboards and hang up your wetsuits – ready for the next morning's guaranteed surf.

Address Washingpool Farm, Main Road, Easter Compton, BS35 5RE, +44 (0)333 0164133, www.thewave.com // Getting there Bus 411, 623 or 625 to Easter Compton; close to junction 17 of the M5 // Hours Daily 6am–7.30pm, but hours subject to change, so check website // Ages 4+

TIP: You can see Wales from The Wave. Why not make a trip over the Severn Bridge?

103_ WICKER WHALES

Magnificent creatures of the deep

'Welcome two Whales' says a hand-painted sign on the Portway, the road next to the River Avon that connects Hotwells with Avonmouth. No, it's not a spelling mistake, even though Wales is less than 10 miles away from this spot as the crow flies. There are actually two magnificent creatures of the deep here, a humpback whale just poking her head up, and a blue whale diving down with her tail in the air.

These two life-size whales are a reminder of when Bristol was the European Green Capital in 2015. Made from Somerset willow, the animals were originally installed in Millennium Square, where they were surrounded by 70,000 'upcycled' plastic bottles from the Bristol 10k and Bath Half Marathon races, representing the threat of plastic pollution in the world's oceans, particularly plastic bags and food and drink packaging.

> TIP: A giant wicker nose can be found on the side of a house on Roslyn Road in Redland.

Another artwork that was part of the Green Capital celebrations was less of a success. *Treesong* was meant to make music from the sound of nuts falling from a beech tree on the Downs, but there were no nuts!

After Bristol's year as Green Capital, the whales were moved to a new home in a nature reserve next to the Portway. Bennett's Patch and White's Paddock Nature Reserve – known as the 'people's nature reserve' – was created by Avon Wildlife Trust. Much of the steel skeleton of the whales can now be seen, but there are still patches of wicker among the plants now growing over them. The idea is that the willow sculptures eventually become part of the landscape here as nature takes over.

Address Bennett's Patch and White's Paddock, Portway, BS9 1RQ, www.bristolwhales.tumblr.com // Getting there Access on foot is through a gate at the corner of Bramble Lane and Bramble Drive, Sneyd Park, BS9 1RD // Hours Accessible 24 hours // Ages 4+

104_ WILD PLACE PROJECT

Conservation in action

For the first time in almost 190 years, visitors to Bristol in 2023 are not able to take a trip to Bristol Zoo at its historic home in Clifton. Over the decades, the zoo and its animal attractions have delighted visitors. But the world's oldest zoo outside a capital city closed for the last time in September 2022, with homes due to be built on the site.

The closure of the old Bristol Zoo is not the end of its story, however, with its sister site Wild Place due to change its name to Bristol Zoo within a few years. For now, visitors are welcome at Wild Place, whose spacious grounds out in the Gloucestershire countryside away

from the city (within easy distance of The Wave (see ch. 102) and Aerospace Bristol (see ch. 29)) enables it to host larger animals in a natural setting rather than a man-made environment.

Head to Bear Wood to find European brown bears, wolves, lynxes and wolverines, with raised walkways winding through ancient woodland giving a bird's-eye view of the magnificent creatures below. Bears are not part of the deal, but keep an eye out for the return of the junior keeper experience for children aged from 6 to 15, with youngsters able to accompany a keeper on their duties, including the opportunity to feed some of the animals.

If the animals around Wild Place have inspired you, try the Leap of Faith course, which as well as having that leap to catch hold of a bag up to 12 feet away, also has a range of climbing challenges such as the rope race, a bear climbing wall and a totem pole.

TIP: Enjoy the kids' menu at nearby Mollie's Diner, inspired by the retro American roadside pit-stop.

Address Blackhorse Hill, BS10 7TP, +44 (0)117 4285602, www.wildplace.org.uk // Getting there Bus 2 to Easter Compton Golf Club, or 1 & 2 to Catbrain Lane // Hours Daily 10am–5pm // Ages 2+

105_ WILDFLOWER MEADOW

From Greta to long grass

When Greta Thunberg came to Bristol in February 2020, thousands of people packed onto College Green to hear the then 17-year-old speak. 'I will not stand aside and watch, I will not be silent while the world is on fire. Will you?' demanded the Swedish activist. 'World leaders are behaving like children, so it falls on us to be the adults in the room. It should not be this way.'

After her speech, Greta led the gathered throng on a march through the city in the pouring rain. The dampness of the day meant, however, that the grass on College Green turned into a mud bath, leading to a crowdfunder to restore it immediately being launched. After a few days, £15,000 had been raised. But despite some scaremongering and media headlines, it was found that the grass had not been badly damaged and would grow back.

It was then decided by the organisers of the original fundraising appeal and Bristol Youth Strike 4 Climate, the organisers of the event featuring Greta, that the money should be spent creating a green space for nature in the heart of the city. Working with the Bristol & Bath Parks Foundation, a wildflower meadow was planted – the results of which today even taller children can hide behind as dozens of native species provide a rich new habitat for pollinators.

> **TIP:** A concrete section of College Green is one of Bristol's most popular skating spots.

'Nature will thrive anywhere if we let it, even in a bustling city green space' says the information board in front of the miniature meadow. A tapestry of rebellious wildflowers is always waiting to spring up across paths, parks and walls.

Address College Green,
BS1 5TJ // Getting there
The meadow is in front of
the cathedral's north-
eastern corner, off Trinity
Street // Hours Accessible
24 hours // Ages 3+

106_ WILLS TOWER TOURS

Get a bird's-eye view of Bristol

Peregrine falcons nest on the outside of the Wills Memorial Building tower, which has an unrivalled vantage point close to the top of Park Street. You might see the remains of some pigeons and seagulls that have come off second best with these birds during your tour. Look out for a model of a human skeleton too on your way up to the top of the tower, where you can get a matchless view of Bristol below.

The walk to the top of the tower – a symbol of the University of Bristol – is not for the faint hearted. There is a total of 345 steps up some winding narrow passageways not usually accessible to the public. The climb to the roof is just part of this 90-minute tour, which raises money for Bristol Children's Hospital. Find out about famous students of the university, from *Gruffalo* creator Julia Donaldson (French & drama) to actor Jason Isaacs (law) who played Lucius Malfoy in the *Harry Potter* movies. Walk inside the Great Hall and original university library, which both have the feel of Hogwarts.

> TIP: Nearby is one of Bristol's best named thoroughfares, There And Back Again Lane.

You will be able to sit on the chair that Winston Churchill sat on when he was chancellor of the university, once presiding over a graduation ceremony in the great hall whose roof had been destroyed by German incendiary bombs. You will meet Great George – or Gert George in Bristolian vernacular. This is one of the biggest bells in England, and you will get up close and personal to hear it bong. You will also learn how this magnificent building was built with money made from chocolate and tobacco.

Address Queen's Road, Clifton, BS8 1RJ, +44 (0)117 9545219, www.bristol.ac.uk/university/visit/tower-tours // Getting there Short walk from top of Park Street // Hours Sat 11am & 1pm // Ages 8+

107_WILLSBRIDGE MILL

From frogs to fairies

Have you heard the expression, 'as calm as a mill pond'? Have you ever wondered where it comes from? Well, you're in luck at Willsbridge Mill, which has its own mill pond. Once upon a time, these pools of water provided the power to make the wheels of mills turn. Today, this pond delights children as they pond dip for tadpoles, newts, frogs and other wildlife. You might also spot a dragonfly, and you will definitely see a luxuriating lizard made out of sparkling mosaic tiles.

Follow the path down from the pond to Siston Brook, where some decking allows you to get almost above the water. Bring wellies or jelly shoes so you can paddle in the stream. Or balance on the rocks to try to get to the other side. On a calm day, it's amazing to think that a devastating flood struck here in July 1968, with Siston Brook becoming a roaring torrent that seriously damaged the mill and surrounding area. The mill may no longer be working, but you can still walk inside the building and imagine the days when a giant waterwheel used to turn here.

TIP: Famous astronomer Sir Bernard Lovell was born in nearby Oldland Common, with the secondary school in the village named after him.

Head to the café if you get peckish (the Jammie Dodger blondies are particularly delicious) and then explore the rest of the site, which includes a wildlife trail and even a fairy wood with a magical grotto. Regular forest school sessions for children aged one to seven take place near the mill pond, with a working waterwheel model in the old mill where you can also find out more about some of the people who used to work here, in calm and not so calm times.

Address Bath Road, Longwell Green, BS30 6EX, +44 (0)117 9323852, www.willsbridgemill.com // Getting there Bus 17 or 45; if driving, use the car park at Long Beach Road and walk through the valley // Hours Accessible 24 hours // Ages 1+

Forest
School
Area

108_ WINDOWS TO THE PAST

Time-travelling on King Street

Bristol Old Vic holds the distinction of being the oldest continually operating theatre in the English-speaking world. That the theatre is still here today is something of a miracle. Many other theatres constructed around the time that it was built only lasted a few years before burning down, but the Old Vic has remained standing for more than 250 years.

Despite that long history, it has only been in the last few years that the theatre itself has been visible from King Street, thanks to a new glass foyer, and the outside of the historic auditorium has been opened up for the first time. When it first opened, this theatre was illegal. If you wanted to see a show, you had to knock on the door of a house belonging to one Mr Foote, then wander through his back yard to get into the venue that was hidden from prying eyes.

Those earliest days of the theatre can be recreated in a bespoke augmented reality app called Windows to the Past that lets you immerse yourself in the history of the building through the centuries, and discover the drama developing through every renovation. Use your own iPad or pick one up from the box office to become a time traveller.

Architectural plans, committee minutes and photographs have been used to recreate what the foyer looked like during the 1770s, 1860s, 1910s and 1970s. Portals appear on your screen as you approach them in real life. Step into the past, and while you're in the Old Vic, be sure to catch a show in the main theatre or in the studio downstairs, or grab a bite to eat in the café which is part of today's foyer.

Address King Street, BS1 4ED, +44 (0)117 9877877, www.bristololdvic.org.uk // Getting there 5-minute walk from fountains // Hours Box office open Mon–Sat 1–6pm // Ages 5+

TIP: Harry and Meghan, the Duke and Duchess of Sussex, went on an official walk-about on King Street in 2019.

109_ WOOD CARVINGS

If you go down to the woods today…

A buzzard with a monumental wingspan flies gracefully through the air. Nearby, an owl keeps watch, while underneath her a trio of bats hang upside down, and a few hedgehogs shelter under some leaves. Look closely and you might see a dormouse or two, or perhaps a deer, a ladybird, a bumblebee or a butterfly – maybe even a badger.

These are all birds, animals and insects that make their home in this historic parkland close to the M32, but if you are not lucky enough to see them in the flesh (or should that be in the fur?), an artist has enabled you to enjoy their company all year round. Andy O'Neill is a chainsaw artist who has combined his two previous careers as a graphic designer and tree surgeon to create these unique works of art sculpted out of fallen trees.

The Bristol artist has been inspired by the nature around him – Andy's own favourite piece of his in Stoke Park is the giant conkers and conker bench that are positioned in the shade of an ancient horse chestnut tree. Catch a glimpse of them for the first time and you might think that your eyes are playing tricks on you, such is their scale and attention to detail.

Each of Andy's pieces took him around three weeks to create over the course of 2022, with passing walkers and cyclists able to watch each of the works taking shape. Step away from reality to visit a fairy castle with giant mushrooms and a fearsome fire-breathing dragon. This fantasy sculpture was inspired by drawings by children from nearby Stoke Park Primary School.

Address Between Long Wood and Hermitage Wood, Stoke Park, BS16 1AU (what3words: salad.bar.sing) // Getting there Bus 10 or 11 to Romney Avenue; 15-minute walk from Filton Abbey Wood railway station // Hours Accessible 24 hours // Ages 2+

TIP: Lockleaze Adventure Playground – known as The Vench – has been entertaining kids for almost 50 years.

110_ZARA'S CHOCOLATES

Bristol's very own Willy Wonka

Did you know that the chocolate bar was invented in Bristol? The first-ever Easter egg in the UK was also made in Bristol by the same company, Fry's, whose factory on Union Street once dominated the city centre until it moved out to Keynsham and later became part of Cadbury's.

Look out for old adverts for Fry's in Zara's Chocolates, who continue to make delicious confectionery in Bristol. You can even learn how to be a chocolatier yourself (if you're 16 or over) where you can choose either to mould bars, or make truffles or pralines. While you're here, try the ice cream taco or ice cream sundae – both made for sharing.

The eponymous Zara Naracott of Zara's Chocolates was named by schoolmates in her secondary school yearbook as 'Most likely to become Willy Wonka'. And it has come true! Her shop and café on North Street are also her workshop, where you can watch Zara and her own Oompa Loompas at work. Willy Wonka himself would be impressed with one particular creation on the shelves at Zara's: a sprout. Okay, if you bite into it, what appears to be the green vegetable is actually chocolate; but it wouldn't look out of place on the dinner table at Christmas among the turkey and all the trimmings.

Christmas is a time when the shop is at its most magical, with plenty of choices perfect for presents. And of course, what's the true meaning of Easter but chocolate? Easter eggs here continue the tradition that started in Bristol, and no other eggs are as delicious as those made here by Zara and her small team.

TIP: A giant mural above Zara's Chocolates forms part of the Six Sisters – each one painted by a different female artist.

228

Address 200 North Street, Southville, BS3 1JF, +44 (0)117 9636956, www.zaraschocolates.com // Getting there Opposite North Street Green; catch the 24 bus to North Street or a 15-minute walk from Wapping Wharf // Hours Tue–Sat 10am–5pm // Ages 2+

111_ THE ZIG-ZAG

Zig-a-zig-ah

Hewn out of the hillside, rocks from the side of the Avon Gorge form part of the perimeter of some of the Zig-Zag path, several jutting through the stone walls. They are a reminder of when this was literally a cliff-face. Not many cities in the world have such an awe-inspiring geological feature within walking distance of its centre. The rock here is carboniferous limestone, with the gorge thought to have formed during the Pleistocene period between 1.8 million and 11,700 years ago.

But back to the Zig-Zag, which connects Clifton above with Hotwells below, once the site of hot baths to rival neighbouring Bath. One theory why this path is serpentine-shaped is so that horses could climb the steep incline, but it must have changed since those early days as there are now around a dozen steps towards the bottom, meaning the path is unsuitable for buggies and wheelchairs. As you try to position yourself vertically, despite the gradient, stop to admire the tenacity of the trees that hug the cliff face, some even using the rocks to balance both their trunks and their roots on.

The simplest derivation of how Clifton got its name is a shortening of 'cliff town', and the Zig-Zag is not the only pathway that clings to the hillside. These thoroughfares may be steep, but they are also joyfully car-free. Promenade down Polygon Lane, gallivant down Goldney Lane, wind up White Hart Steps and head down Hinton Lane for an incredible view of the retaining wall of Windsor Terrace protruding into the Avon Gorge above.

Address Top of path close to Hotel du Vin, Sion Hill, Clifton, BS8 4LD //
Getting there 2-minute walk from Clifton Suspension Bridge // Hours
Accessible 24 hours // Ages 4+

TIP: Turn right at the top of the Zig-Zag to find the former Clifton Rocks Railway.

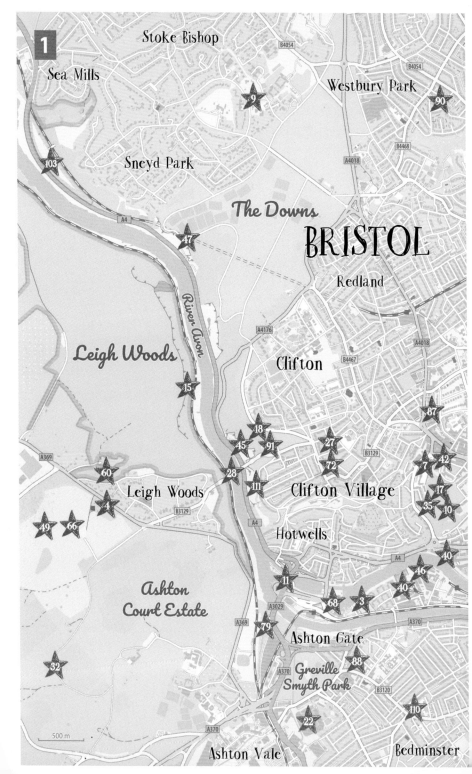

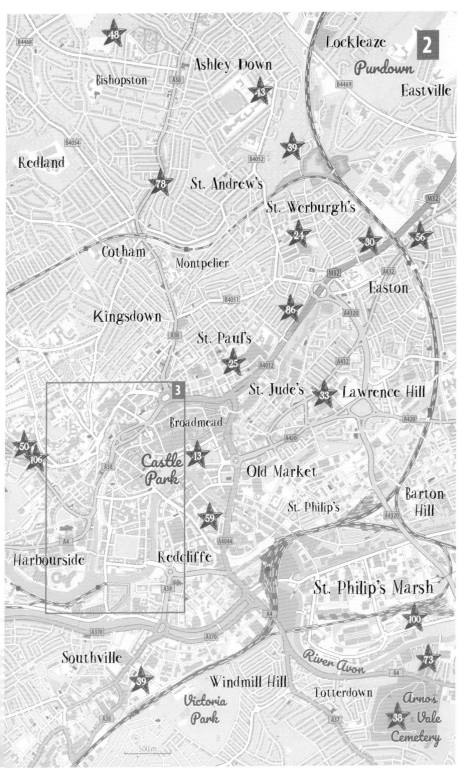

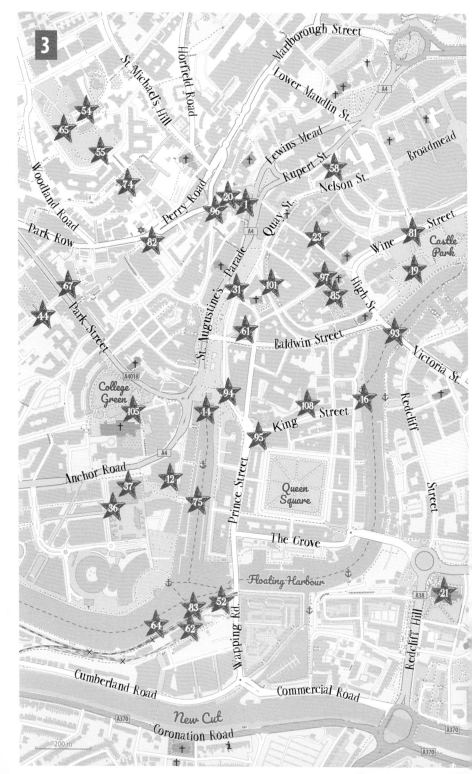

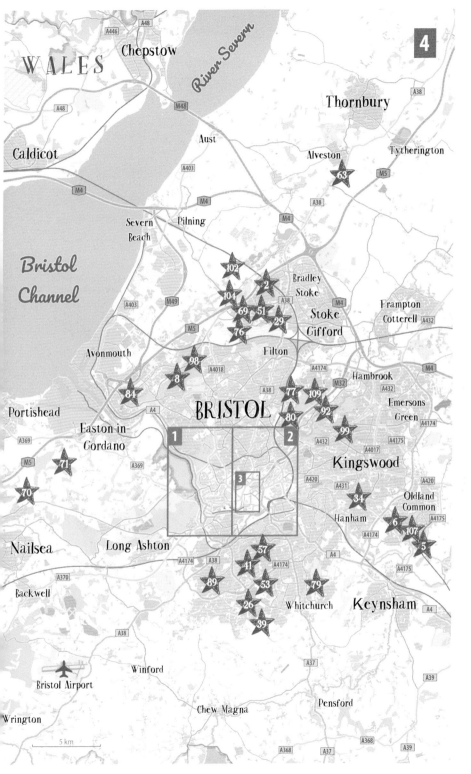

Martin Booth, Barbara Evripidou
111 Places in Bristol
That You Shouldn't Miss
ISBN 978-3-7408-1612-4

John Sykes, Birgit Weber
111 Places in London
That You Shouldn't Miss
ISBN 978-3-7408-1644-5

Julian Treuherz,
Peter de Figueiredo
111 Places in Manchester
That You Shouldnɑt Miss
ISBN 978-3-7408- 1862-3

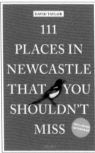

David Taylor
111 Places in Newcastle
That You Shouldn't Miss
ISBN 978-3-7408-1043-6

Katherine Bebo, Oliver Smith
111 Places in Bournemouth
That You Shouldnɑt Miss
ISBN 978-3-7408- 1166-2

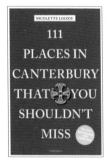

Nicolette Loizou
111 Places in Canterbury
That You Shouldn't Miss
ISBN 978-3-7408-0899-0

Rob Ganley, Ian Williams
111 Places in Coventry
That You Shouldn't Miss
ISBN 978-3-7408-1044-3

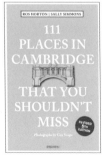

Rosalind Horton,
Sally Simmons, Guy Snape
111 Places in Cambridge
That You Shouldn't Miss
ISBN 978-3-7408-1285-0

Michael Glover,
Richard Anderson
111 Places in Sheffield
That You Shouldnɑt Miss
ISBN 978-3-7408-1728-2

THANKS

Mersina and Lois: what adventures we have had during the writing of this book! I look forward to many more escapades ahead, maybe even outside of Bristol. (p.s. Please stop growing up so fast.) Jo: thank you for being so wonderful, so understanding and so supportive. Although words are meant to be the tools of my trade, I could never find enough ways to say thank you. We have made our life together in Bristol and I am so lucky to have you by my side.

Thank you to everyone who made this book possible, especially the ever-brilliant Barbara Evripidou (we somehow did it again!); my ever-forgiving editor Ros Horton; and the ever-excellent team at Emons who showed so much trust in Babs and me.

Thank you to my mum and dad, Shelagh and Tony, for making my first memories in Bristol. Thank you to the numerous friends who have given me words of encouragement, especially Tash Ebbs at Small Street Espresso and Jonny Simpson at Full Court Press. Thank you to my colleagues at Bristol 24/7, especially Ben Wright for granting my request of a much-needed four-week sabbatical to go on a busman's holiday to write a large chunk of this book in the hot summer of 2022. And special thanks to Emily and Gwen for their love of alpacas; Eugene Byrne for his knowledge of Purdown Percy; Flo Stewart and everyone at The Wave for a wonderful stay; Wills Memorial Building tour guide extraordinaire Gary Nott; Jo and Alice at Lyme Regis Library; Kate Iles for her story of St Blaise; Laura Hilton and Etain O'Shea at the Clifton Suspension Bridge; Lucy and Alfie Holloway for being my soft play buddies; Mary Milton and Luke Merrett for their Bumpsy detective work; Mia, Rachel, Jono, Allan and all the brilliant team at Circomedia; Philippa Walker at the University of Bristol; Rose Logan for her climbing skills; St Mary Redcliffe for their kind permission to reproduce the quote about the chaotic pendulum; Steve and Christina at Laser Fusion; Zoe Fawcett and the team at Padel4All Lockleaze; everyone at Yuup for turning me from guidebook writer into tour guide; and to everyone on Twitter for taking part in the poll to officially decide the name of the slidey rock.

This book was written in Bristol at the Arnolfini, Artist Residence, Boston Tea Party, Bristol Loaf, Burra, Central Library, Chapter & Holmes, Cloakroom, Dareshack, Fed 303, Full Court Press, Grain Barge, Little Victories, Millennium Square, New Cut, The Park, Small Goods, Small Street Espresso, Society, Spicer & Cole, Watershed, Waterstones and Wogan Coffee; in Lyme Regis at Amid Giants & Idols, Costa and Lyme Regis Library; in Brighton in Small Batch, Artist Residence and Wolfox; and in Bath in Colonna & Small's.

Martin Booth

Huge thanks to Martin and Joanna Booth (and the girls) for their continual support throughout the process. You are both lush and have been great as always. And thank you to our publishers Emons for supporting us in bringing out a second book.

A special mention to Dave at 20th Century Flicks, the Ahh Toots team, All-Aboard Watersports, Bristol Blue Glass, Circomedia, Alice at the Clifton Observatory, Craig at Wolfridge Alpacas, Jo at Be Weird Be Wild Be Wonderful, Hayley at Boing!, the Bristol Bears, Chance & Counters, the Bristol School of Gymnastics, Tim at Campus Skatepark, the Children's Scrapstore, Flying Saucers, SS *Great Britain*, the staff at the harbour train, Jeevan's, Laser Fusion, Mrs Potts Chocolate House, Rory at Noah's Ark Zoo Farm, Oakham

Treasures, Padel4all Lockleaze, Kerstin & Nigel at Playfull Toy Shop, Lucy at Golden Hill Community Garden, Rhona at Scribble & Sketch, Skyboat Café, Square Food Foundation, Andy at Beast, Lucy at Wild Place, David & Fran at Oliver's, Cat at the George Müller Museum, Suzi at Filwood Crazy Golf, The Wave, Gary at Wills Memorial Building, Willsbridge Mill and last but not least, Amanda and Harriet at the Bristol Old Vic for the best Wednesday ever! I'm sure I may have unintentionally missed some people out but I really do thank you all.

To my dear friends who have supported me: especially Jenny, Sangee, Jackie, Joolie, Emily, Lucy, Rachel, Vicki and Freia. Also Poppy for giving up a Saturday for a huge adventure.

Thank you to my ever-supportive, amazing family, Mum, Anna, Pete, Carina, Leo, Amelia and Artemis. I am so lucky, you are the best. Thank you to my partner, Paul. I love that you get me and I've loved being with you on this journey. Thank you to my kids, Theo and Anna, for being so wonderful and understanding, especially all the times that 'mum is out shooting for the book again'!

Finally, a massive thank you to all the children, parents, grandparents and carers who gave their time and energy to getting these photos. It's been so much fun photographing you all. This book would not have looked so good without you in it.

Barbara Evripidou

Martin Booth is a journalist and author who lives in Bristol with his wife, Joanna, and their two daughters, Mersina and Lois. He spends more time on two wheels than two feet, and devotes too much time advocating for segregated cycle lanes. His two daughters worked out when they were still very young that when he's not cycling, he will usually be found having either a coffee or a beer. He is also a tour guide, leading regular walking tours of the Old City and Castle Park with Yuup. Follow Martin on Twitter for all things Bristol and more: @beardedjourno.

Barbara Evripidou is an award-winning photographer with three decades of experience. As a former press photographer, her images have been published in national newspapers and she has worked across the world. The highlight of her career was working with the British Army in Bosnia, covering the efforts to rebuild the country. These days she focuses on PR, portrait and commercial work. When she's not got a camera in her hand you can find her at a metal gig, at the cinema or exploring Bristol where she lives with her children, Theo and Anna. Find out more at firstavenuephotography.com.